Atholl CENTRE

Atholl CENTRE

Vegetarian Cooking for You

Marguerite Patten

Vegetarian Cooking for You

HAMLYN

Acknowledgements
The following photographs kindly supplied by:
Birds (Dream Topping): page 87
British Sugar Bureau: page 90
Carmel Produce Information Bureau: pages 63, 75, 86
Dutch Dairy Bureau: pages 19, 43, 47
Kelloggs: pages 83, 91
Marmite: pages 22-23
McDougalls Home Baking Bureau: page 39
Olives from Spain: pages 51, 54-55

Line illustrations by Kim Elliott

Published by
Hamlyn Publishing
Astronaut House, Feltham, Middlesex, England
© Copyright Hamlyn Publishing 1978
a division of The Hamlyn Publishing Group Limited
Revised edition 1980
Fifth impresion 1984
ISBN 0 600 32228 9

Printed in Spain by Cayfosa. Sta. Perpètua de Mogoda · Barcelona
Phototypeset in England by Photocomp Limited, Birmingham
Dep. Legal B-30115-1984

Contents

Useful Facts and Figures

Notes on metrication

In this book quantities are given in metric, Imperial and American measures. Exact conversion from Imperial to metric measures does not usually give very convenient working quantities and so the metric measures have been rounded off into units of 25 grams. The table below shows the recommended equivalents.

Ounces	Approx g to nearest whole figure	Recommended conversion to nearest unit of 25
1	28	25
2	57	50
3	85	75
4	113	100
5	142	150
6	170	175
7	198	200
8	227	225
9	255	250
10	283	275
11	312	300
12	340	350
13	368	375
14	396	400
15	425	425
16 (1 lb)	454	450
17	482	475
18	510	500
19	539	550
20 (1¼ lb)	567	575

Note: When converting quantities over 20 oz first add the appropriate figures in the centre column, then adjust to the nearest unit of 25. As a general guide, 1 kg (1000 g) equals 2·2 lb or about 2 lb 3 oz. This method of conversion gives good results in nearly all cases, although in certain pastry and cake recipes a more accurate conversion is necessary to produce a balanced recipe.

Liquid measures The millilitre has been used in this book and the following table gives a few examples.

Imperial	Approx ml to nearest whole figure	Recommended ml
¼ pint	142	150 ml
½ pint	283	300 ml
¾ pint	425	450 ml
1 pint	567	600 ml
1½ pints	851	900 ml
1¾ pints	992	1000 ml (1 litre)

Spoon measures All spoon measures given in this book are level unless otherwise stated.

Can sizes At present, cans are marked with the exact (usually to the nearest whole number) metric equivalent of the Imperial weight of the contents, so we have followed this practice when giving can sizes.

Flour Unless specified, either plain or self-raising flour, wholemeal, white or brown, can be used in the recipes.

Seasoned flour This is flour seasoned with salt and pepper, usually used to coat foods prior to frying.

Freezing Where there is no mention of freezing in a recipe it means that the dish is unsuitable or rather unsatisfactory for freezing.

Choice of ingredients Where recipes state alternatives e.g. 'butter or margarine', this indicates that the ingredient mentioned first will give the better result in that particular recipe. But of course a vegetarian fat, such as margarine, can be used instead.

Oven temperatures

The table below gives recommended equivalents.

	°C	°F	Gas Mark
Very cool	110	225	$\frac{1}{4}$
	120	250	$\frac{1}{2}$
Cool	140	275	1
	150	300	2
Moderate	160	325	3
	180	350	4
Moderately hot	190	375	5
	200	400	6
Hot	220	425	7
	230	450	8
Very hot	240	475	9

Notes for American and Australian users

In America the 8-oz measuring cup is used. In Australia metric measures are now used in conjunction with the standard 250-ml measuring cup. The Imperial pint, used in Britain and Australia, is 20 fl oz, while the American pint is 16 fl oz. It is important to remember that the Australian tablespoon differs from both the British and American tablespoons; the table below gives a comparison. The British standard tablespoon, which has been used throughout this book, holds 17·7 ml, the American 14·2 ml, and the Australian 20 ml. A teaspoon holds approximately 5 ml in all three countries.

British	American	Australian
1 teaspoon	1 teaspoon	1 teaspoon
1 tablespoon	1 tablespoon	1 tablespoon
2 tablespoons	3 tablespoons	2 tablespoons
$3\frac{1}{2}$ tablespoons	4 tablespoons	3 tablespoons
4 tablespoons	5 tablespoons	$3\frac{1}{2}$ tablespoons

Note: When making any of the recipes in this book, only follow one set of measures as they are not interchangeable.

The list below gives some American equivalents or substitutes for terms and ingredients used in this book.

British	American
baking tin	baking pan
baking tray	baking sheet
black treacle	molasses
cling film	saran wrap
cocktail stick	toothpick
cream, double	heavy cream
cream, single	light cream
dried milk powder	milk solids
fat	shortening
flour, plain	all-purpose flour
flour, self-raising	all-purpose flour sifted with baking powder
flour, wholemeal	wholewheat flour
foil	aluminum foil
frying pan	skillet
glacé cherries	candied cherries
greaseproof paper	wax paper
grill	broil, broiler
hard-boiled eggs	hard-cooked eggs
haricot beans	navy beans
kitchen paper	paper towels
mince	grind
mixer, liquidiser	mixer, blender
packet	package
pastry, shortcrust	basic pie dough
piping bag	pastry bag
piping tube	nozzle, tip
polythene	plastic
spring onions	scallions
stoned	pitted
sugar, demerara	light brown sugar
sugar, icing	confectioners' sugar
sultanas	seedless white raisins
whisk	whip, beat

Introduction

This book is intended for all households, not just people who are strictly vegetarian. The ever-increasing price of meat has made most of us decide to change our menus from time to time. This is a good thing, for it means we not only have a chance to save money but we also add greater variety to our meals.

There are many ways in which one can obtain an adequate amount of protein without eating meat. You can make delicious and satisfying meals based on cheese and egg; you will find a wide selection in this book. You can also use nuts; these are health-giving, interesting and versatile protein foods.

Remember that bread is one of the most economical ways of adding protein to the diet, although obviously one must eat bread, or products based on flour, in reasonable amounts, if one does not want to put on extra weight.

Investigate the range of products stocked by Health Food Stores, for in these specialist shops are first-rate nuts, nut products and interesting meatless products.

Many of the dishes in this book use economical and very appetising natural vegetable proteins (generally referred to as 'pulses'). The vegetables rich in protein are lentils, beans of all kinds (including soya beans) and peas. Many people consider these just as a vegetable to serve as an accompaniment, but they can form the basis of a great variety of new and unusual main dishes.

As this is a book from which you can plan complete menus, I have included a section on desserts and puddings, chosen for their suitability for a vegetarian diet.

I hope both vegetarians and non-vegetarians will enjoy using the recipes.

Marguerite Patten

Good Beginnings

The first course of a meal can be varied and full of interest. Choose dishes based on fruit, vegetables and eggs. Small portions of rice and pasta dishes are excellent if the main course is a light one. Cheese also can be included in hors d'oeuvre as well as main dishes.

Cheese and Grapefruit Salad

Illustrated on page 11
Serves 4

Metric·Imperial	American
2 grapefruit	2 grapefruit
½ red or green pepper	½ red or green pepper
175 g/6 oz Cheddar cheese, diced	1 cup diced Cheddar cheese
grapefruit juice	grapefruit juice
1 tablespoon olive oil	1 tablespoon olive oil
sugar (optional)	sugar (optional)
salt and pepper	salt and pepper
To garnish	**To garnish**
lettuce	lettuce

Halve the grapefruit on a plate. Remove the segments carefully, put into a basin and discard any pips; cut away the skin. Chop the red or green pepper, discard the core and seeds and mix with the grapefruit. Add the diced cheese.

Pour the juice from the grapefruit into a separate basin, blend with the olive oil, sugar, salt and pepper. Pour the dressing over the cheese mixture. Leave for about 30 minutes for the dressing to flavour the other ingredients. Line the halved grapefruit cases with lettuce and pile the salad in the centre.

Freezing This cannot be frozen.

Variations
Use orange segments and serve in sundae glasses.

Top halved peaches with grated cheese or fill centres of pineapple rings with grated cheese blended with mayonnaise.

9

Avocado Rarebit

Serves 3

Metric · Imperial	American
3 slices bread or soft rolls	3 slices bread or soft rolls
little butter	little butter
1 large avocado	1 large avocado
175 g/6 oz Cheddar cheese, grated	1½ cups grated Cheddar cheese
To garnish	**To garnish**
25 g/1 oz peanuts	good ⅛ cup peanuts
2 tomatoes	2 tomatoes

Toast the bread or halve and toast the rolls. Spread with the butter. Halve the avocado, remove the stone and skin and cut the flesh into wafer-thin slices. Top the bread or rolls with most of the slices, save a few for garnish, and top with the cheese. Put under the grill and heat until the cheese melts. Top the toasted cheese mixture with the remaining avocado slices and sprinkle the peanuts over the top. Slice the tomatoes and arrange round the dish to serve.

Avocado and Grapefruit Salad

Serves 4

Metric · Imperial	American
¼ lettuce heart	¼ lettuce heart
2 medium grapefruit	2 medium grapefruit
1 large avocado	1 large avocado
1 tablespoon lemon juice	1 tablespoon lemon juice

Avocados are a good source of protein and grapefruit adds vitamin C.

Shred the lettuce heart and put into cocktail glasses or on small dishes. Cut away the peel and pith from the grapefruit and discard. Cut the fruit segments from the skin, discarding any pips. Halve the avocado, remove the stone and peel the fruit, slice the pulp. Mix with the lemon juice and grapefruit segments; spoon on the lettuce.

Freezing This cannot be frozen.

Variation

Avocado cocktail Prepare the ingredients as above, but cut the avocado and grapefruit segments into small pieces. Mix with mayonnaise, flavoured with a little tomato purée, and serve on the bed of lettuce.

Grapefruit Surprise

Serves 4

Metric · Imperial	American
2 large grapefruit	2 large grapefruit
2 rings fresh or canned pineapple	2 rings fresh or canned pineapple
2 tablespoons dry sherry	3 tablespoons dry sherry
25 g/1 oz butter	2 tablespoons butter
25 g/1 oz brown sugar	2 tablespoons brown sugar
¼ teaspoon ground cinnamon	½ teaspoon ground cinnamon

Halve the grapefruit, remove the segments. Chop the pineapple, mix with the grapefruit and return to the grapefruit halves, moisten with the sherry. Mix together the butter, brown sugar and cinnamon. Spread over the top of the fruit and heat under a hot grill for 3 minutes. Serve hot.

Variation

Mix other fruit, such as diced melon, seedless grapes or sliced banana with the grapefruit segments.

Cheese and Grapefruit Salad (see page 9)

Stuffed Pears

Serves 4

Metric·Imperial	American
4 small or 2 large dessert pears	4 small or 2 large dessert pears
For the vinaigrette dressing	**For the vinaigrette dressing**
2 tablespoons salad oil	3 tablespoons salad oil
2 tablespoons lemon juice	3 tablespoons lemon juice
salt and pepper	salt and pepper
pinch sugar	pinch sugar
For the filling	**For the filling**
150 ml/¼ pint natural yogurt	⅔ cup plain yogurt
25 g/1 oz walnuts, chopped	¼ cup chopped walnuts
175 g/6 oz Cheddar cheese, grated	1½ cups grated Cheddar cheese
50 g/2 oz sultanas	scant ½ cup seedless white raisins
pinch cayenne pepper	pinch cayenne pepper
To garnish	**To garnish**
lettuce	lettuce
lemon	lemon

Peel, halve and core the pears. Put into a dish. Blend the ingredients for the dressing and pour over the pears. Leave for 15 minutes, turning once. Mix the yogurt with the nuts, cheese, sultanas and cayenne. Lift the pears from the dressing, top with the cheese mixture and place on a bed of lettuce leaves. Slice the lemon then twist the slices, and decorate the pears.

Variations

Use cream cheese instead of grated cheese and only enough yogurt to make a softer consistency.

Stuffed avocados Use avocados in place of dessert pears.

Potted Cheese

Serves 4-6

Metric·Imperial	American
225 g/8 oz cheese	½ lb cheese
50 g/2 oz butter or margarine	¼ cup butter or margarine
1 tablespoon dry sherry or a little lemon juice	1 tablespoon dry sherry or a little lemon juice
pinch grated nutmeg	pinch grated nutmeg
salt and pepper	salt and pepper

Grate hard cheese, or crumble then mash softer cheeses. It is possible to use all kinds of cheese in this recipe or mix cheeses, so this is a practical way to use up leftover pieces of cheese. Melt the butter or margarine, add half to the cheese, together with the sherry or lemon juice, nutmeg and seasoning to taste. Spoon into small dishes and top with the remaining melted butter. Leave until the coating on top is hard.

Serve with crisp toast or fresh bread.

Freezing This will keep in a refrigerator for 2-3 weeks or about 6 weeks in a freezer.

Variations

Add chopped fresh herbs to the cheese mixture.

Add peeled diced cucumber to the cheese mixture (this is less suitable for freezing as the cucumber would lose its crisp texture).

Do not imagine that a pâté cannot be prepared from ingredients other than liver; there are a great variety of basic ingredients from which you can choose. Quantities are not given in all recipes as the proportions of ingredients are a matter of personal taste. Each of these pâtés can be served on a bed of lettuce, accompanied by toast and butter.

Avocado Pâté

Illustrated on page 71

Halve ripe avocados, remove the stones, then the pulp from the skins and put into a basin. Add lemon juice immediately (you need at least 1 tablespoon to each avocado) to keep the flesh from discolouring. Add a little oil, then flavouring to taste; this can be a small amount of crushed garlic or chopped chives; a little finely chopped fresh tarragon; an equal amount of sieved cottage cheese or a small quantity of crumbled Danish Blue cheese, plus seasoning.

Bean Pâté

Soak 100 g/4 oz (U.S. generous ½ cup) haricot beans in water to cover for about 12 hours. Tip the beans and liquid into a pan; add 1-2 peeled and chopped onions, 1-2 peeled crushed cloves of garlic; a small bunch of mixed fresh herbs or a good pinch of dried herbs, salt, pepper and a pinch of dry mustard to taste. Simmer steadily until the beans are tender and the liquid absorbed; you need to watch carefully towards the end of the cooking time. If any surplus liquid is left then discard this. Sieve or mash the beans, adding a little chopped parsley, lemon juice and oil to taste.

Savoury Carrot Pâté

The crispness of raw carrot makes a pleasing contrast to the soft texture of the egg and cottage cheese mixture. This is very good if you are trying to lose weight, as it is low in calories but full of flavour.

Hard-boil, shell and chop 2 eggs. Put into a basin or liquidiser. Sieve 175 g/6 oz (U.S. ¾ cup) cottage cheese, add to the eggs, together with 4 tablespoons (U.S. 5 tablespoons) yogurt, salt, garlic salt, black and cayenne pepper to taste. Pound or liquidise until smooth. Finely grate 2-3 raw carrots, add to the pâté mixture, together with 1 tablespoon chopped parsley and 2 tablespoons (U.S. 3 tablespoons) chopped stuffed olives.

Lentil Pâté

Follow the directions for the Bean Pâté, but use lentils instead of haricot beans.

Vegetable Pâtés

Many vegetables can be cooked with onions and garlic together with herbs and flavourings to taste, until they are just tender, then sieved, mashed or liquidised to produce a smooth mixture. This can be blended with a little cream, lemon juice and more fresh herbs.

Freezing All these pâtés will freeze for about 1 month. The garlic tends to lose some of its potency.

Overleaf left: Spaghetti Milanaise (see page 61)
Overleaf right: Tomato Cups (see page 16)

Salads for Hors d'oeuvre

Many salads are ideal for a meal starter. Serve rather smaller portions than when planning the salad to accompany a main dish.

Tomato Cups

Illustrated on page 15
Serves 4

Select 4 large ripe firm tomatoes. Cut a slice from the end opposite where the stalk grew (this makes certain the tomatoes stand upright). Scoop out the tomato pulp with a teaspoon, chop this and the 4 slices of tomato. Blend with 2 tablespoons (U.S. 3 tablespoons) finely chopped cucumber, 1 tablespoon chopped olives, 1 tablespoon chopped chives and seasoning. Spoon into the tomato cases. Top with a good layer of grated cheese. Stand in an ovenproof dish and bake for 10-12 minutes just above the centre of a moderately hot oven (200°C, 400°F, Gas Mark 6). Top and garnish with parsley and serve with a green salad.

Stuffed Mushrooms

Serves 4

Mushrooms make a delicious start to a meal; they can be filled in various ways. Use 12 large mushrooms to make a starter for 4 people. Wash then dry the mushrooms; remove the stalks and chop these finely; do not peel the mushroom caps. The stuffing is pressed against the under side of the mushrooms.

Parmesan Mushrooms

Peel and chop 1 medium onion; fry in 25 g/1 oz (U.S. 2 tablespoons) hot butter or margarine; add 50 g/2 oz (U.S. 1 cup) soft breadcrumbs, 50 g/2 oz (U.S. ½ cup) grated Parmesan cheese, 1 teaspoon capers, the chopped mushroom stalks and an egg. Season, combine the mixture thoroughly and press into the mushroom caps. Put these into a well greased ovenproof dish. Top with a little more grated cheese and small knobs of butter or margarine and bake for 10-15 minutes towards the top of a moderately hot oven (200°C, 400°F, Gas Mark 6). Serve hot with a fresh tomato purée made by simmering 4-5 skinned and chopped tomatoes with a peeled and grated onion, seasoning to taste, ½ teaspoon chopped oregano and 3-4 tablespoons white wine or water.

Creole Mushrooms

Peel and chop 2 large onions and 1 clove garlic. Dice ½ green pepper very finely; skin and chop 2 tomatoes. Heat 2 tablespoons (U.S. 3 tablespoons) oil in a pan, fry the onions and garlic until soft, then add the pepper and tomatoes. Continue cooking until the mixture becomes a thick purée. Add the chopped mushroom stalks, 25 g/1 oz (U.S. ½ cup) fresh breadcrumbs and seasoning to taste. Press firmly into the mushroom caps. Top with a little grated cheese and bake for 10 minutes towards the top of a moderately hot oven (200°C, 400°F, Gas Mark 6).

Soups

A soup can either be an interesting beginning to a meal or it can form a meal in itself, if it contains sufficiently sustaining and nutritious ingredients.

You will find a selection of both kinds of soups in this chapter. If you want to adapt any of your own favourite recipes to become more substantial and nutritious, there are various ways in which it may be done:

1 Top the cooked soup with cheese just before serving. This can be grated hard cheese, or it can be spoonfuls of cottage or cream cheese.

2 Use rather less water, or vegetable stock, than the recipe advises and make up the extra quantity with milk. Be careful about using milk if the dish contains acid ingredients like tomatoes, for the mixture can curdle.

3 Add some of the high protein vegetables to the soup – lentils, peas or beans. You can thicken the soup with these vegetables instead of the usual flour or cornflour.

4 Creamy soups can become more nourishing if you beat an egg, or egg yolk, with a little liquid and whisk this into the hot, but not boiling, liquid just before serving. Simmer the soup gently for a few minutes, after adding the egg, but do not boil so there is no fear of it separating.

Do not imagine that all soups must be served hot. I have included recipes that are delicious cold or even lightly iced.

The cold soup looks attractive if served in glasses or chilled soup cups. The rim of the soup cup can be dipped in water, then into finely chopped parsley.

To add Flavour to Soup

A good soup is full of flavour and you obtain this by the wise use of seasoning (not just ordinary salt and pepper, but celery salt, paprika or cayenne), by the generous use of suitable herbs, and by making certain the initial stock has flavour. In this particular book it will be a stock from vegetables. Yeast extract can be added and will not only increase the vitamin content but will give an interesting taste as well.

To Serve Soups

Top the cooked or cold soup with chopped herbs, yogurt, crisp croûtons of fried or toasted bread, or chopped nuts.

Vegetable Soup

Serves 4-6

Metric·Imperial	American
350 g/12 oz mixed vegetables, i.e. root vegetables with tomatoes, mushrooms, peas, etc. or use just one vegetable, such as onions, carrots, etc.	¾ lb mixed vegetables, i.e. root vegetables with tomatoes, mushrooms, peas, etc. or use just one vegetable such as onions, carrots, etc.
900 ml/1½ pints water or vegetable stock	3¾ cups water or vegetable stock
yeast extract to taste	yeast extract to taste
salt and pepper	salt and pepper
To garnish	**To garnish**
chopped parsley	chopped parsley

Prepare the vegetables, cut into small dice or grate coarsely to save cooking time and so retain the maximum vitamins. Bring the water to the boil, add a little yeast extract and seasoning, then drop in the vegetables and boil fairly quickly until just tender. Taste and add more yeast extract and seasoning if desired. Serve topped with the parsley.

This is a good basic soup that can be varied throughout the year, using vegetables in season. It can be sieved or liquidised to make a smooth purée, and topped with cheese if desired.

Freezing Cool, then pack. This soup keeps well for 2-3 months. You could use less liquid to conserve space, then add the extra water when reheating.

Cauliflower Soup

Serves 4-6

Slice 1 large leek and fry gently in 50 g/2 oz (U.S. ¼ cup) butter until soft. Stir in 25 g/1 oz (U.S. ¼ cup) flour, add 600 ml/1 pint (U.S. 2½ cups) vegetable stock, water or milk. Bring to the boil, cook, stirring well, until the liquid thickens slightly. Divide a medium cauliflower into sprigs, or use a 340-g/12-oz packet of frozen cauliflower. Add to the sauce, season, cook until the cauliflower is soft. Sieve or liquidise to give a smooth purée soup, then reheat. Top with single cream and chopped parsley.

Freezing This soup freezes well for up to 3 months.

Variation

Add 100 g/4 oz (U.S. 1 cup) grated cheese to the soup just before serving.

Peanut Soup

Illustrated opposite

Serves 6

Put 3 tablespoons (U.S. 4 tablespoons) smooth peanut butter, 50 g/2 oz (U.S. ¼ cup) light brown sugar and 300 ml/½ pint (U.S. 1¼ cups) milk into a saucepan. Heat very gently until the peanut butter and sugar have melted. Chop 1 medium onion and toss in 25 g/1 oz (U.S. 2 tablespoons) butter until soft. Add 450 ml/¾ pint (U.S. 2 cups) vegetable stock, or water flavoured with a little yeast extract, the peanut butter mixture, 175 g/6 oz (U.S. 1½ cups) salted peanuts, the contents of 198-g/7-oz can of sweetcorn and salt and black pepper to taste. Heat thoroughly. Add 225 g/8 oz (U.S. 2 cups) grated Gouda cheese just before serving. Warm gently for a few minutes only. Serve with slices of Gouda Tea Bread (see page 92).

Peanut Soup (see above); Gouda Tea Bread (see page 92)

Chestnut Soup

Serves 4-6

Metric·Imperial	American
450 g/1 lb chestnuts	1 lb chestnuts
600 ml/1 pint water	2½ cups water
50 g/2 oz margarine or butter	¼ cup margarine or butter
300 ml/½ pint milk	1¼ cups milk
salt and pepper	salt and pepper
1 teaspoon sugar	1 teaspoon sugar
To garnish	**To garnish**
few chopped chives	few chopped chives

Wash the chestnuts and make a slit in the skins. Put into a pan with enough water to cover and simmer for about 10 minutes. Strain, discard this water and skin the chestnuts while they are hot. Return to the pan with the 600 ml/1 pint (U.S. 2½ cups) water and simmer until tender, this takes about 35-45 minutes. Sieve the nuts or blend in the liquidiser. Return the purée to the pan, add the margarine or butter, milk, seasoning and sugar, then reheat. Top with the chives.

Freezing This soup freezes well for about 3 months.

Variations

The recipe above is a very bland one; you can add chopped onion, a crushed clove of garlic and a teaspoon of yeast extract to give more flavour.

Bean and chestnut soup Soak 100 g/4 oz (U.S. generous ½ cup) haricot beans overnight, then simmer until nearly soft, add the peeled chestnuts to the beans and the liquid in the pan and continue as the basic recipe or the variation below.

Tomato chestnut soup Use the basic recipe, adding 1 small chopped onion and 4 skinned chopped tomatoes.

Celery and Peanut Soup

Serves 4-6

Metric·Imperial	American
1 head celery	1 bunch celery
1·15 litres/2 pints water	5 cups water
little yeast extract	little yeast extract
salt and pepper	salt and pepper
100-175 g/4-6 oz peanut butter	½-¾ cup peanut butter
40 g/1½ oz wholemeal flour	¼ cup plus 2 tablespoons wholewheat flour
To garnish	**To garnish**
fresh or salted peanuts	fresh or salted peanuts
sliced tomatoes	sliced tomatoes

Dice the washed celery neatly, chop a few of the tender green leaves. Bring most of the water to the boil, add the celery (not the leaves), the yeast extract and seasoning. Cover the pan and cook steadily for 15 minutes. Stir in the peanut butter and the flour, mixed with the remaining water. Stir over a moderate heat until thickened and smooth. Top with peanuts and thinly sliced rings of raw or cooked tomato, and the celery leaves.

Variation

Creamy celery soup Use only 900 ml/1½ pints (U.S. 3¾ cups) water and mix 300 ml/½ pint (U.S. 1¼ cups) milk with the flour and stir into the soup until thickened and smooth. Do not allow to boil after adding the tomato slices to this version or the mixture may curdle.

Lentil Soup

Serves 4-6

Metric·Imperial	American
225 g/8 oz lentils	1 cup lentils
2 medium onions	2 medium onions
2 medium carrots	2 medium carrots
1 medium dessert apple	1 medium dessert apple
600 ml/1 pint water	2½ cups water
small bunch parsley	small bunch parsley
1 teaspoon chopped fresh thyme	1 teaspoon chopped fresh thyme
salt and pepper	salt and pepper
25 g/1 oz margarine or butter	2 tablespoons margarine or butter
15 g/½ oz flour	2 tablespoons all-purpose flour
300 ml/½ pint milk	1¼ cups milk
To garnish	**To garnish**
2 tomatoes	2 tomatoes
little chopped parsley	little chopped parsley

It shortens the cooking time if the lentils are soaked overnight in water to cover; this can then be used as part of the liquid in the soup. If you intend to sieve the soup, the peeled onions, carrots and apple can be coarsely chopped; otherwise it looks more attractive if they are grated.

Simmer the lentils in the water with the vegetables, apple, herbs and seasoning until tender. This takes about 1 hour if the lentils have been soaked, but 1¼-1½ hours if they have been put straight into the pan. Remove the bunch of parsley. Sieve or liquidise the mixture, then return it to the pan. Add the margarine or butter and the flour mixed with the milk. Stir over a moderate heat until thickened. Skin and chop the tomatoes. Serve the soup topped with the tomatoes and parsley.

Freezing This soup freezes well, although the purée may tend to separate during storage and will need whisking hard. The flour and milk is better if added when reheating. Use within 2-3 months.

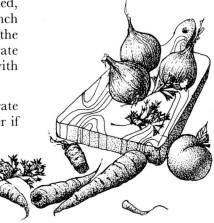

Lentil and Tomato Chowder

Serves 4-6

Metric·Imperial	American
450 g/1 lb lentils	2 cups lentils
1·15 litres/2 pints water	5 cups water
little yeast extract	little yeast extract
450 g/1 lb tomatoes	1 lb tomatoes
2 onions	2 onions
1-2 cloves garlic	1-2 cloves garlic
100-175 g/4-6 oz peanut butter	½-¾ cup peanut butter
salt and pepper	salt and pepper

Put the lentils with the water and yeast extract to flavour into a large saucepan. Add the tomatoes, there is no need to skin or chop these if you intend sieving or liquidising the soup. Peel and chop the onions and garlic, add with the peanut butter and seasoning. Simmer steadily for 1¼-1½ hours unless you have soaked the lentils, when they will take just 1 hour. Either serve at once or sieve or liquidise the mixture and reheat.

Freezing Although garlic tends to lose some flavour in freezing this soup can be frozen for 2-3 weeks.

Variation
Omit peanut butter and use 50 g/2 oz (U.S. ¼ cup) margarine or butter.

Overleaf: Leeks au Gratin (see page 41); French Onion Soup (see page 24); Vegetable Shepherd's Pie (see page 80)

Dutch Bean Broth

Serves 4-6

Metric · Imperial	American
100 g/4 oz haricot beans	generous ½ cup navy beans
1·15 litres/2 pints water	5 cups water
3 medium onions	3 medium onions
salt and pepper	salt and pepper
To garnish	**To garnish**
little margarine or butter	little margarine or butter
little cream or natural yogurt	little cream or plain yogurt
chopped parsley	chopped parsley

Put the beans to soak in the water overnight. This soup can be served with the whole beans, in which case chop the onions finely, but if you intend to sieve or liquidise the mixture then they can be coarsely chopped. Simmer the beans and onions gently until tender, seasoning the mixture well; this takes about 1½-2 hours, but can be done in a pressure cooker at H/15 lb pressure for about 15 minutes; in which case reduce the amount of water slightly, as this will not evaporate in the same way as in a saucepan for the longer cooking time. Sieve the soup or liquidise, if you want a smooth purée soup, then return to the saucepan. Reheat. Top each serving with a small knob of margarine or butter and a spoonful of cream or yogurt and chopped parsley.

Freezing This soup freezes well whether sieved or not. The purée version may separate during storage and need whisking hard on reheating. Use within 2-3 months.

Variation

Tomato and bean soup Use about 600 ml/1 pint (U.S. 2½ cups) tomato juice instead of the same quantity of water. Top the soup with grated cheese.

French Onion Soup

Illustrated on pages 22-23
Serves 8-10

This soup is a pleasant combination of onions and cheese. Peel and thinly slice 675 g/1½ lb (U.S. 1½ lb) onions, and 2 cloves garlic. Toss in 75 g/3 oz (U.S. 6 tablespoons) butter or margarine, then add 1·75 litres/3 pints (U.S. 7½ cups) brown stock, flavoured with a generous amount of yeast extract (this goes well with the onion flavour). Cover the pan, simmer steadily for 30 minutes, taste and add seasoning if desired. Top with slices of French bread or toast and a layer of grated cheese.

Cheese Soup

Serves 4-6

Metric · Imperial	American
50 g/2 oz butter or margarine	¼ cup butter or margarine
2 medium onions, chopped	2 medium onions, chopped
40 g/1½ oz flour	¼ cup plus 2 tablespoons all-purpose flour
750 ml/1¼ pints milk or milk and water	3 cups milk or milk and water
175 g/6 oz Cheddar or other good cooking cheese, grated	1½ cups grated Cheddar or other good cooking cheese
salt and pepper	salt and pepper

Heat the butter or margarine in a pan and fry the onions for a few minutes; take care they do not discolour. Stir in the flour, then gradually add the milk, or milk and water. Bring to the boil and stir until thickened. Lower the heat and simmer for 5-6 minutes, stirring once or twice. Add the cheese just before serving and season to taste. It is advisable not to cook for any length of time after adding the cheese as it could become tough and you cannot judge the seasoning until the cheese has been put in.

Freezing This freezes reasonably well but may need whisking very hard as it is reheated. Do not boil the soup quickly but thaw and heat without boiling.

Variations
This soup is capable of many variations, for cheese blends with most tastes. You can add a variety of cooked vegetables and just heat these for a few minutes.

Add several peeled and grated raw carrots and/or a diced green and red pepper to the soup just before adding the cheese; this makes sure they retain their crisp texture.

Add 1-2 tablespoons yeast extract to the soup.

Add 2-3 tablespoons chopped fresh herbs.

Overleaf left: Harlequin Cheese Soup (see page 28)
Overleaf right: Egg Salad (see page 29)

Low calorie Dishes

Vegetarians, like all groups of people, may encounter problems in controlling their weight. Unfortunately, most cheeses, while invaluable to provide protein and calcium, are fairly high in calories and therefore something to restrict while you are trying to lose weight. Remember cottage cheese has a high protein value, so substitute this for other cheese in salads, in a soup (as in the recipe below which is illustrated on page 26), or in a sauce. Eggs are an important food when on a diet; poach these in water, without margarine; use a 'non-stick' pan for making omelettes, so cutting down on the amount of fat used. Hard-boiled eggs are extremely satisfying, so they can be used as the basis for a number of salads (see opposite).

Harlequin Cheese Soup

Illustrated on page 26
Serves 4-6

Metric·Imperial	American
450 g/1 lb cottage cheese	2 cups cottage cheese
600 ml/1 pint low-fat yogurt	2½ cups low-fat yogurt
salt and pepper	salt and pepper
1-2 tomatoes	1-2 tomatoes
1 small red pepper	1 small red pepper
2 tablespoons chopped parsley	3 tablespoons chopped parsley
2 tablespoons chopped chives	3 tablespoons chopped chives
1 small leek or 2-3 spring onions	1 small leek or 2-3 scallions

Either rub the cheese through a sieve or put into a liquidiser or food processor. Add the yogurt and beat or liquidise until smooth. Add salt and pepper to taste. Skin and finely dice the tomatoes, chop the pepper into small pieces, discard the core and seeds, and add the parsley and chives. Discard all the tough ends of the stems from the leek or spring onions and chop the white part finely. Put all these ingredients into the soup and chill.

Freezing This could be frozen for 2-3 weeks, but omit the pepper, leek or onions until defrosted, for these should retain their firm crisp texture.

Variations
A little finely grated lemon rind and juice can be added if desired.
    If you prefer this soup hot, put into the top of a double saucepan or a basin over boiling water, then heat.

White Sauce

This particular sauce is fairly high in calories because of the fat and flour content. To make it less fattening, use skimmed milk or half milk and half vegetable stock, where applicable.

To make the sauce, heat 25 g/1 oz (U.S. 2 tablespoons) butter or margarine in a saucepan. Stir in 25 g/1 oz (U.S. ¼ cup) flour (or you could use 15 g/½ oz (U.S. 2 tablespoons) cornflour, for although this has almost the same calories as flour, you use only half the quantity to achieve the same result in thickening a liquid). Gradually add 300 ml/½ pint (U.S. 1¼ cups) milk or other liquid (see above). Bring to the boil and cook until thickened, then season to taste.

Flavouring for White Sauce

Cheese sauce Add 50-100 g/2-4 oz (U.S. ½-1 cup) grated Cheddar or other good cooking cheese to the thickened white sauce; do not overheat this sauce. Use double the amount of cottage cheese (this should be sieved) and stir into the hot liquid, or see the special low-calorie sauce below.

Hard-boiled egg sauce Add 1-2 shelled and finely chopped hard-boiled eggs to the sauce.

Herb sauces Add 1-2 tablespoons freshly chopped fennel, dill or parsley to the white sauce.

Low-calorie White Sauce

Yogurt can be used to make a low-calorie sauce.

Blend 300 ml/½ pint (U.S. 1¼ cups) yogurt with the yolks of 2 eggs, a little salt and pepper. Put into a basin, or the top of a double saucepan, and cook until thickened. Whisk during the cooking period. Milk could be used instead of yogurt. This can be flavoured as the White Sauce (see above).

Low-calorie Salad Dressings

It is the oil content that makes most salad dressings so high in calories, so dress salads in well-seasoned lemon juice instead of an oil and lemon dressing, or use well-seasoned yogurt instead of mayonnaise. Add a little lemon juice to yogurt, or make the sauce with yogurt as above, allow to cool, stirring well, then flavour with lemon juice, salt, pepper and a little made mustard.

Egg Salads

Illustrated on page 27

When hard-boiling eggs remember to time the cooking process carefully. If you place the eggs into cold water and bring this to the boil, then allow only about 8-9 minutes, for the eggs start to cook as the water comes to the boil. If placing into boiling water, allow just 10 minutes. Always crack the shell and plunge the eggs into cold water as soon as cooked.

There are many ways of making the egg yolk more interesting: halve the eggs, remove the yolks, blend with a little low-calorie dressing or mayonnaise, then flavour with curry powder or curry paste; cooked or canned sieved asparagus tips; finely chopped red pepper; mixed herbs. Spoon back into the white cases, place on the bed of salad and top with a dressing or mayonnaise.

Overleaf left: Cheese and Onion Custard (see page 32)
Overleaf right: Walnut Cheese Dolmas (see page 32)

Cheese and Onion Custard

Illustrated on page 30
Serves 3-4

Metric·Imperial	American
350 g/12 oz onions	¾ lb onions
salt and pepper	salt and pepper
150 ml/¼ pint onion stock (see method)	⅔ cup onion stock (see method)
2 egg yolks	2 egg yolks
2 eggs	2 eggs
450 ml/¾ pint skimmed milk	scant 2 cups skimmed milk
50 g/2 oz Cheddar cheese, finely grated	½ cup finely grated Cheddar cheese
To garnish	**To garnish**
1-2 tomatoes	1-2 tomatoes
parsley	parsley

Peel and slice the onions, and cut the rings into quarters. Put into a saucepan with 300 ml/½ pint (U.S. 1¼ cups) water, salt and pepper to taste. Cover the pan, simmer for 10-15 minutes or until the onions are *nearly*, but not quite, tender. Strain the liquid saving 150 ml/¼ pint (U.S. ⅔ cup). Blend with the egg yolks and whole eggs. Heat the milk, pour over the egg mixture, and add a little extra seasoning. Spoon the onions and cheese into an ovenproof dish, then strain the custard over this mixture; stand in a bain-marie (tin of cold water). Bake in the centre of a cool oven (150°C, 300°F, Gas Mark 2) for approximately 1¼ hours until just firm to the touch. Slice the tomatoes, then put them on to the custard with a sprig of parsley. Serve hot or cold.

Freezing This custard does not freeze well; if you do want to freeze the mixture, use half full-cream milk and half double cream.

Variations
Add a crushed clove garlic and mixed chopped fresh herbs to the custard.
Use up to 175 g/6 oz (U.S. 1½ cups) grated cheese.

Walnut Cheese Dolmas

Illustrated on page 31
Serves 3-4

Metric·Imperial	American
6-8 large but tender cabbage leaves	6-8 large but tender cabbage leaves
salt and pepper	salt and pepper
150 ml/¼ pint cabbage stock (see method)	⅔ cup cabbage stock (see method)
For the filling	**For the filling**
50 g/2 oz cooked rice or soft breadcrumbs	good ⅓ cup cooked rice or 1 cup soft breadcrumbs
50 g/2 oz Cheddar cheese, finely grated	½ cup finely grated Cheddar cheese
50 g/2 oz walnuts, finely chopped	½ cup finely chopped walnuts
1 tablespoon chopped parsley	1 tablespoon chopped parsley
1 tablespoon chopped chives	1 tablespoon chopped chives
25-50 g/1-2 oz margarine, melted	2-4 tablespoons melted margarine
1 egg	1 egg
For the topping	**For the topping**
White or Cheese Sauce (see page 29)	White or Cheese Sauce (see page 29)

Wash and drain the cabbage leaves. Bring just over 150 ml/¼ pint (U.S. ⅔ cup) water to the boil and add a little salt and pepper. Put in the cabbage leaves. Boil for 1½-2 minutes (just long enough to soften the leaves) and lift from the liquid. Cool slightly and spread each cabbage leaf flat.

Mix the ingredients for the stuffing together, adding salt and pepper to taste. Divide the stuffing between the leaves, then fold them to enclose the filling. Put them into a casserole with the cabbage stock, cover tightly and cook in the centre of a very moderate oven (160°C, 325°F, Gas Mark 3) for 35-40 minutes. Meanwhile make the sauce. Lift the Dolmas from the liquid on to a hot dish; top with the sauce.

Freezing The Dolmas freeze well in the cabbage stock for 3 months. Reheat and strain.

Packed Meals

Vegetarians, like most people, may find it difficult to plan dishes that can be carried. The suggestions on this page and pages 34-36 are intended for picnics or other occasions when you need to transport food. Most of the dishes are, however, very good served hot as well as cold.

Egg and Tomato Patties

Illustrated on page 35
Makes 8

Metric·Imperial For the filling	American For the filling
2 small onions	2 small onions
4 large tomatoes	4 large tomatoes
25 g/1 oz margarine	2 tablespoons margarine
50 g/2 oz cooked rice	good ⅓ cup cooked rice
salt and pepper	salt and pepper
1 tablespoon chopped parsley	1 tablespoon chopped parsley
4 eggs	4 eggs
For the pastry	**For the pastry**
350 g/12 oz white or wholemeal flour, preferably plain	3 cups white or wholewheat flour, preferably all-purpose
pinch salt	pinch salt
175 g/6 oz margarine or vegetarian fat	¾ cup margarine or vegetarian fat
water to bind	water to bind
To garnish	**To garnish**
parsley	parsley

Peel and finely chop the onions. Skin and chop the tomatoes. Heat the margarine and fry the onions for 2-3 minutes, then add the tomatoes and cook until a thick pulp. Add the rice, salt, pepper and chopped parsley. Cool slightly. Meanwhile, hard-boil, shell and halve the eggs.

Sift the flour and salt; rub in the margarine or fat and bind with the water. Roll out and use nearly ⅔ of the pastry to line 8 individual deep patty tins. Cut 8 rounds from the remaining pastry. Spoon half the rice mixture into the pastry-lined tins. Top with the eggs, cut side downwards, then the rest of the rice mixture. Damp the edges of the pastry with a little water; put on the pastry lids. Seal and flute the pastry edges. Bake in the centre of a moderately hot oven (200°C, 400°F, Gas Mark 6) for 15-20 minutes until crisp and brown. Garnish with parsley; serve cold with salad. The patties could be carried in the patty tins or in a polythene box. They are also excellent served hot with a Cheese Sauce (see page 29).

Freezing These patties cannot be frozen as the hard-boiled eggs would become tough and inedible.

Cheese Cutlets

Serves 4

Metric·Imperial

40 g/1½ oz margarine
40 g/1½ oz flour
300 ml/½ pint milk
225 g/8 oz Cheddar or Gruyère cheese,
    grated
salt and pepper
little made mustard
2 tablespoons chopped fresh herbs (parsley,
    thyme, chives, sage)
50 g/2 oz soft white or wholemeal
    breadcrumbs

To coat
approximately 25 g/1 oz flour
1 egg
approximately 50 g/2 oz crisp breadcrumbs

For frying
2-3 tablespoons oil

American

3 tablespoons margarine
½ cup plus 2 tablespoons flour
1¼ cups milk
2 cups grated Cheddar or Gruyère
    cheese
salt and pepper
little made mustard
3 tablespoons chopped fresh herbs (parsley,
    thyme, chives, sage)
1 cup soft white or wholewheat
    breadcrumbs

To coat
approximately ¼ cup flour
1 egg
approximately ½ cup crisp breadcrumbs

For frying
3-4 tablespoons oil

Heat the margarine in a saucepan, then add the flour; stir over a low heat for 2-3 minutes. Gradually blend in the milk, bring to the boil and cook until a thick sauce. Add the cheese, salt, pepper, mustard, herbs and breadcrumbs. Mix thoroughly, and place 8 portions on a plate. Chill for a short time in the refrigerator until the mixture is sufficiently firm to handle. Form into small cutlet shapes. Coat in the flour, beaten egg and breadcrumbs. Heat the oil in a large frying pan and fry the cutlets for about 2 minutes until crisp and brown, then turn and crisp on the second side. Drain on absorbent paper.

To carry on a picnic, place on fresh absorbent paper in a polythene box. Serve with salad.

Freezing Open freeze then wrap; use within 3 months.

Variations
Cooked rice or cooked chopped pasta could be used instead of breadcrumbs.

Cheese and onion cutlets Peel and finely chop 2 medium onions. Heat 50 g/ 2 oz (U.S. ¼ cup) margarine in a saucepan. Add the onions and cook gently until tender; stir from time to time. Continue as the Cheese Cutlets above. You can add 50 g/2 oz (U.S. ½ cup) chopped walnuts to make an interesting variation.

Cheese and potato cutlets Use 200 ml/7½ fl oz (U.S. 1 cup) milk only for the sauce. Substitute 100 g/4 oz (U.S. ½ cup) cooked and mashed potatoes for the breadcrumbs. These are better served hot. The Tomato Sauce, under Spaghetti Milanaise (see page 61), is an excellent accompaniment. Add 2-3 tablespoons (U.S. 3-4 tablespoons) finely chopped watercress to the mixture.

Cheese and tomato cutlets Use tomato juice or fresh tomato purée in place of milk.

Egg cutlets Hard-boil, shell and chop 4 eggs. Use in place of the grated cheese. You can add 2-3 chopped hard-boiled eggs to the Cheese Cutlets.

Egg and Tomato Patties (see page 32)

Summer-time Pie

Serves 6

For the filling

40 g/1½ oz margarine
40 g/1½ oz flour
200 ml/7½ fl oz milk
175 g/6 oz Cheddar cheese, finely grated
salt and pepper
1 teaspoon made mustard
350 g/12 oz *lightly cooked** summer
   vegetables, e.g. peas, beans, cauliflower,
   young carrots, etc.

For the pastry

350 g/12 oz white or wholemeal flour,
   preferably plain
salt, pepper, pinch dry mustard
150 g/5 oz margarine or vegetarian fat
40 g/1½ oz finely grated Parmesan
   cheese
1 egg yolk
water to bind

To glaze

1 egg or a little milk

American

For the filling

3 tablespoons margarine
¼ cup plus 2 tablespoons flour
1 cup milk
1½ cups finely grated Cheddar cheese
salt and pepper
1 teaspoon made mustard
¾ lb *lightly cooked** summer vegetables,
   e.g. peas, beans, cauliflower, young
   carrots, etc.

For the pastry

3 cups white or wholewheat flour,
   preferably all-purpose
salt, pepper, pinch dry mustard
⅝ cup margarine or vegetarian fat
3 tablespoons finely grated Parmesan
   cheese
1 egg yolk
water to bind

To glaze

1 egg or a little milk

*The vegetables should retain much of their original texture

Heat the margarine in a saucepan, stir in the flour and cook over a low heat for 2-3 minutes. Gradually blend in the milk and stir over a low heat until a very thick binding sauce (a panada). Add the cheese, salt, pepper and the mustard. Tip the vegetables into the hot sauce, stir gently to blend, then allow to cool.

Sift the flour with the seasonings, rub in the margarine or fat, add the cheese, egg yolk and enough water to bind. Roll out and use just over half the pastry to line an 18-20-cm/7-8-inch square sandwich tin. Spoon the vegetable mixture into the pastry case. Roll out the remaining pastry into a square to fit the tin and cut several pastry leaves for garnish. Damp the edges of the pastry, place the top pastry in position, seal the edges very firmly, then flute. Score the pastry to form diagonal lines and brush with beaten egg or milk; place the 'leaves' in position and glaze these.

Bake the pie in the centre of a moderately hot oven (200°C, 400°F, Gas Mark 6) for 20 minutes, lower the heat slightly and cook for a further 5-10 minutes. Serve cold with Salad Provençal (below). It is easy to carry this picnic dish in the baking tin.

If serving hot, make extra Cheese Sauce (see page 29), and serve this with the pie.

Freezing This pie freezes well for up to 3 months.

Salad Provençal

Serves 6

Peel and thinly slice a good-sized onion, slice about ⅓ of a cucumber (this can be peeled if desired) and several tomatoes; dice the pulp from a small red and a small green pepper (discarding the cores and seeds). Crush 1 clove garlic. Blend 3 tablespoons (U.S. 4 tablespoons) olive oil, 1½ tablespoons (U.S. 2 tablespoons) lemon juice with the garlic, salt, pepper and a pinch sugar. Arrange the salad ingredients on a bed of lettuce; top with the dressing. Carry the salad in a polythene box and the dressing in a screw-topped jar.

Cheese Dishes

Remember that all types of cheese add protein and calcium to your diet. Encourage children to eat as much cheese as possible, for this helps to build sound bones and strong teeth.

When you cook with cheese choose a good cooking variety. Some of the easily obtainable cheeses that are good for cooking are Cheddar, Cheshire, Dutch Edam or Gouda, Gruyère, Emmenthal and Parmesan.

If you shop wisely and vary the cheeses used in cooking, salads, or other dishes, these should never become monotonous.

When trying to lose weight use more cottage cheese than any other, for this is lower in calories.

Making Pastry

The secret of good pastry is to handle the ingredients as lightly as possible; to keep the dough cool; and to use just the right amount of liquid, for too much makes the pastry rather tough as it cooks and too little means it is almost impossible to handle.

If you have not made pastry with wholemeal flour you will find it gives an excellent result. It is a good idea to sift the flour to lighten it and also to remember that this flour does tend to absorb a *very little* more liquid than white flour. Because of this the pastry may take a little longer in cooking and it might be advisable to use a slightly lower heat to make sure it does not overcook.

As a general rule, shortcrust pastry uses half the quantity of fat to flour with a little cold water to bind. To make, follow the basic method given in the recipe, omitting the extra seasonings.

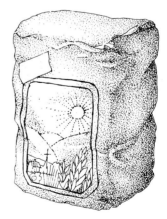

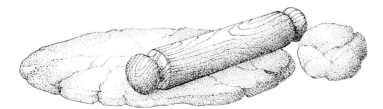

Cornish Cheese Pie

Illustrated opposite
Serves 4-6

Metric·Imperial
For the filling

2 medium potatoes
1-2 medium carrots
50 g/2 oz shelled peas
salt and pepper
1 medium onion
25 g/1 oz margarine
½ teaspoon chopped mixed herbs or thyme or
   2 teaspoons chopped parsley
1 egg (optional)

For the cheese pastry

225 g/8 oz plain flour
pinch salt
1 teaspoon dry mustard
100 g/4 oz vegetarian fat
50-75 g/2-3 oz Cheddar cheese, finely grated
little water

To glaze

egg or milk

American
For the filling

2 medium potatoes
1-2 medium carrots
scant ½ cup shelled peas
salt and pepper
1 medium onion
2 tablespoons margarine
½ teaspoon chopped mixed herbs or thyme or
   2 teaspoons chopped parsley
1 egg (optional)

For the cheese pastry

2 cups all-purpose flour
pinch salt
1 teaspoon dry mustard
½ cup vegetarian shortening
½-¾ cup finely grated Cheddar cheese
little water

To glaze

egg or milk

Peel and dice the potatoes and carrots. Cook these and the peas in seasoned boiling water until just tender, then strain. Peel and chop the onion, heat the margarine and toss the onion in this. Mix all the filling ingredients well together.

To make the pastry, sift the flour, salt and mustard together. Rub in the fat, until the mixture resembles fine breadcrumbs. Add the cheese. Mix to a firm dough with water. Turn the pastry out on to a lightly floured board and divide in 2 pieces. Roll out one half and use to line a 20-cm/8-inch well-greased ovenproof pie plate. Moisten edges of pastry with water, spoon the vegetable filling in the centre then cover with the remaining pastry, rolled out into a circle slightly larger than the plate. Press the edges well together to seal, cut away any surplus pastry, then flute the edges. Brush the top of the pie with beaten egg or milk and decorate with pastry leaves, cut from the pastry trimmings. Bake the pie in the centre of a hot oven (220°C, 425°F, Gas Mark 7) for 25-30 minutes. Lower the heat after 20 minutes if pastry is browning too quickly. Serve hot or cold with salad.

Freezing This pie freezes well after cooking, use within 2 months.

Variation
Add 100-175 g/4-6 oz (U.S. 1-1½ cups) grated cheese to the filling ingredients.

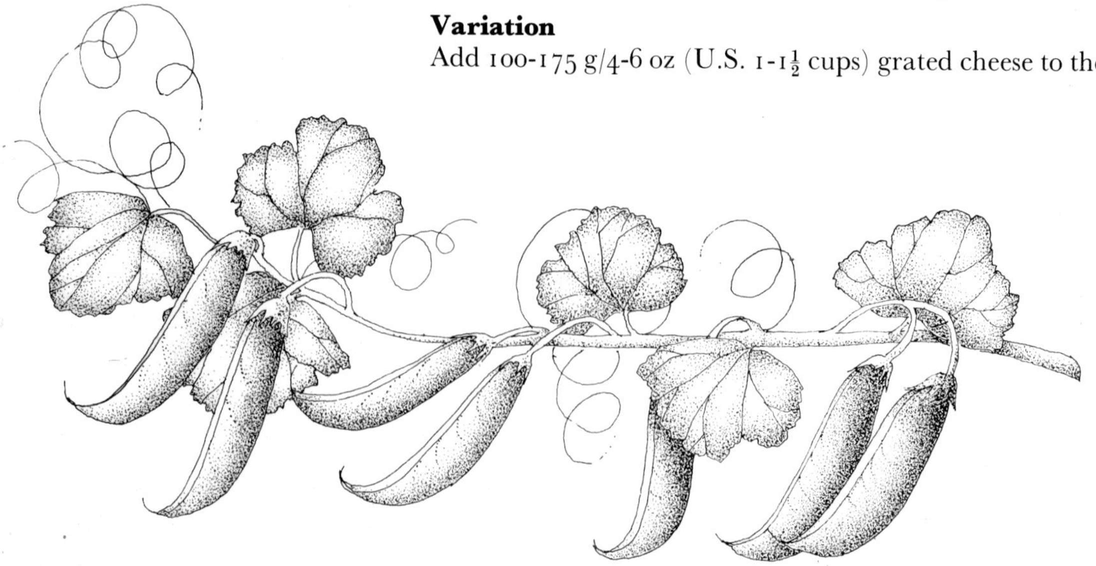

Onion and Mushroom Flan

Illustrated on page 43
Serves 4-6

Metric·Imperial	American
shortcrust pastry, made with 175 g/6 oz plain flour, etc. (see page 37)	basic pie dough made with 1½ cups all-purpose flour, etc. (see page 37)
175 g/6 oz mushrooms	1½ cups mushrooms
2 large onions	2 large onions
50 g/2 oz butter	¼ cup butter
3 eggs	3 eggs
2 tablespoons milk	3 tablespoons milk
salt and pepper	salt and pepper
100 g/4 oz Gouda cheese, grated	1 cup grated Gouda cheese
To garnish	**To garnish**
sprig watercress	sprig watercress

Roll out the pastry and line a 20-cm/8-inch sandwich or flan tin. Bake 'blind' (see page 48) for 10-15 minutes, until the pastry is crisp but not brown. Wash and slice the mushrooms, peel and chop the onions. Heat the butter and fry the onions, then the mushrooms. Put some mushroom slices on one side for garnish. Spoon the remainder of the mushrooms and all the onions into the flan case. Beat the eggs with the milk, add seasoning and cheese. Pour over the vegetables and cook for about 30 minutes in the centre of a moderate oven (180°C, 350°F, Gas Mark 4). Top with the sliced mushrooms and watercress. Serve hot or cold.

Freezing This flan freezes well. Open-freeze, then wrap. Use within 3 months.

Variation
Carrot and mushroom flan Omit the onions, substitute 100 g/4 oz (U.S. 1 cup) peeled and coarsely grated carrot. Fry the mushrooms, as the basic recipe, then add the grated carrots and proceed as above.

Cheese Pudding

Serves 4

This light, soufflé-like pudding makes a satisfying dish. It can be varied in a number of ways, as suggested in the recipe. Use either white or wholemeal breadcrumbs. This dish must be served at once.

Put 450 ml/¾ pint (U.S. scant 2 cups) milk into a saucepan. Add 40 g/1½ oz (U.S. 3 tablespoons) margarine or butter, a pinch of salt and shake of pepper. Heat until the margarine or butter has melted. Add 75 g/3 oz (U.S. 1½ cups) fine soft breadcrumbs and then allow to stand for 15 minutes to soften the crumbs. Beat 3 eggs, stir into the crumb mixture then pour into an 18-20-cm/7-8-inch soufflé dish or ovenproof dish. Bake in the centre of a moderate to moderately hot oven (190-200°C, 375-400°F, Gas Mark 5-6) for approximately 35 minutes or until well risen and firm.

Variations
Use tomato juice in place of milk; cook 1 or 2 onions, sieve or liquidise and use, with the onion stock, in place of milk; add chopped parsley or other herbs to taste.

Cheese and Vegetable Hotpot

Illustrated on page 43
Serves 6

Cook 1 kg/2 lb (U.S. 2 lb) mixed vegetables. Make a cheese sauce (see page 29), but use double quantities. In this recipe Dutch Gouda is ideal. Put the strained vegetables and sauce in layers in a heated flameproof casserole. Top with grated cheese and heat until the topping has melted; garnish with chopped parsley.

Make a cheese sauce (see page 29), but add a little yeast extract for extra flavour and B vitamins. Cook 8-12 small leeks, strain. Put into a flameproof dish, top with the sauce and a layer of grated cheese and soft breadcrumbs. Brown under the grill.

Vegetarian Moussaka

Serves 4-6

Metric·Imperial	American
2 large onions	2 large onions
3 large tomatoes	3 large tomatoes
2 cloves garlic (optional)	2 cloves garlic (optional)
2 medium aubergines	2 medium eggplants
little salt	little salt
4 medium potatoes	4 medium potatoes
100 g/4 oz margarine or vegetarian fat	$\frac{1}{2}$ cup margarine or vegetarian shortening
2 tablespoons oil	3 tablespoons oil
1 (447-g/15$\frac{3}{4}$-oz) can baked beans	1 (15$\frac{3}{4}$-oz) can baked beans
For the sauce	**For the sauce**
50 g/2 oz margarine	$\frac{1}{4}$ cup margarine
50 g/2 oz flour	$\frac{1}{2}$ cup all-purpose flour
600 ml/1 pint milk	2$\frac{1}{2}$ cups milk
225 g/8 oz Cheddar or other cooking cheese, grated	2 cups grated Cheddar or other cooking cheese
$\frac{1}{2}$-1 teaspoon mixed spice	$\frac{1}{2}$-1 teaspoon mixed spice
salt and pepper	salt and pepper
To garnish	**To garnish**
chopped parsley	chopped parsley

Peel and slice the onions, tomatoes and garlic. Wipe the aubergines, but do not peel. If you dislike their somewhat bitter taste score the skin, sprinkle with salt and leave for 15 minutes before slicing. Cut the aubergines and the peeled potatoes into *thin* slices. Heat half the margarine or vegetarian fat and half the oil and toss the aubergines and potatoes in this for several minutes. Remove from the pan, add the rest of the margarine or fat and oil and fry the onions, tomatoes and garlic for 5-6 minutes, mix with the canned beans.

Make the sauce: heat the margarine, stir in the flour, then mix in the milk and bring to the boil, stir until thickened, add the cheese, spice and seasoning, do not cook again. Put one-third of the well seasoned vegetables into an ovenproof casserole, add one-third of the sauce. Continue the layers, ending with a good layer of sauce. Cover the casserole and cook for 1$\frac{1}{4}$ hours in the centre of a moderate oven (160°C, 325°F, Gas Mark 3). Top with parsley.

Freezing This freezes well for 2 months – defrost before reheating.

Variations
Stir 1 or 2 eggs or egg yolks into the sauce, after adding the cheese.

Soya moussaka Omit the canned beans and use canned soya mince or chunks instead.

Moussaka au gratin (illustrated on page 42). Omit the final layer of sauce and cover the last layer of fried aubergines (leaving a border if liked) with sliced tomato, 50 g/2 oz (U.S. 1 cup) fresh breadcrumbs and 50 g/2 oz (U.S. $\frac{1}{2}$ cup) grated cheese. Cook as above. Garnish with watercress sprigs and serve with a mixed green salad.

Overleaf left: Moussaka au Gratin (see above)
Overleaf right: Onion and Mushroom Flan (see page 40);
Cheese and Vegetable Hotpot (see page 40)

Cheese and Onion Loaf

Serves 6

Metric · Imperial

Metric · Imperial	American
50 g/2 oz All-Bran	¾ cup All-Bran
150 ml/¼ pint milk	⅔ cup milk
225 g/8 oz self-raising flour or plain flour mixed with 2 teaspoons baking powder	2 cups all-purpose flour sifted with 2 teaspoons baking powder
pinch salt	pinch salt
pinch cayenne pepper	pinch cayenne pepper
50 g/2 oz margarine	¼ cup margarine
100 g/4 oz cheese, grated	1 cup grated cheese
1 onion	1 onion
To garnish	**To garnish**
tomato slices	tomato slices

Soak the All-Bran in the milk until this is absorbed. Sift the flour, salt and cayenne into a basin. Rub in the margarine. Stir in the cheese, peel and chop the onion and add with the All-Bran mixture; mix together thoroughly. Turn on to a lightly floured board and knead. Press the mixture into a greased 0·5-kg/1-lb loaf tin. Bake in the centre of a moderately hot oven (190°C, 375°F, Gas Mark 5) for about 50 minutes. Turn out, and spread while warm or cold with butter or margarine and serve with a salad or soup.

Freezing This loaf freezes well; use within 2 months.

Variation
If using wholemeal flour use an extra tablespoon of milk.

Celery Cheese Pie

Serves 4

Metric · Imperial	American
1 head celery	1 bunch celery
salt and pepper	salt and pepper
25 g/1 oz margarine	2 tablespoons margarine
25 g/1 oz flour	¼ cup all-purpose flour
150 ml/¼ pint milk	⅔ cup milk
175 g/6 oz cheese, grated	1½ cups grated cheese
2 tablespoons tomato ketchup or purée	3 tablespoons tomato ketchup or paste
1 egg	1 egg
450 g/1 lb mashed potatoes	2 cups mashed potatoes
2 tomatoes	2 tomatoes

Wash, then chop the celery. Cook in boiling salted water until just tender. This takes about 15 minutes. Strain and save 150 ml/¼ pint (U.S. ⅔ cup) stock. Place the celery in an ovenproof dish. Make a white sauce with the margarine, flour, milk and celery stock (see page 29). Season well, stir in most of the cheese and tomato ketchup or purée and lastly the beaten egg – do not allow the sauce to boil. Pour the sauce over the celery. Top with mashed potato, then the rest of the cheese and sliced tomatoes. Cook for approximately 20-25 minutes towards the top of a moderately hot oven (190°C, 375°F, Gas Mark 5).

Serve hot with a green salad.

Cheese Charlotte

Serves 4-6

Metric·Imperial	American
3 eggs	3 eggs
1 teaspoon made mustard	1 teaspoon made mustard
salt and pepper	salt and pepper
600 ml/1 pint milk	2½ cups milk
4-5 slices buttered bread	4-5 slices buttered bread
100-175 g/4-6 oz cheese, grated	1-1½ cups grated cheese

Beat the eggs, add the mustard, seasoning and milk. Cut the buttered bread into small squares. Put a layer of bread in an ovenproof dish, and most of the cheese. Pour over the savoury custard mixture, and top with the remaining cheese. Bake in the centre of a moderately hot oven (190°C, 375°F, Gas Mark 5) until golden brown and puffy – about 45 minutes.

Serve hot with a salad or green vegetables.

Variations

Egg, onion and cheese charlotte Hard-boil 4 eggs, boil and chop 3-4 onions. Arrange the sliced eggs and chopped onions in layers with the bread, etc. Cook as above.

Mushroom charlotte Slice 100 g/4 oz (U.S. 1 cup) mushrooms very thinly. Toss for 2-3 minutes in 25 g/1 oz (U.S. 2 tablespoons) hot butter; add to the mixture.

Vegetable and cheese charlotte Omit the bread and use sliced cooked potatoes instead, or add layers of cooked diced mixed vegetables to the recipe above. Avoid using tomatoes, for they might make the mixture curdle in cooking. Children would enjoy some baked beans, which give flavour and additional protein to the charlotte.

Savoury Stuffed Onions

Serves 4

Metric·Imperial	American
4 medium onions	4 medium onions
salt and pepper	salt and pepper
1 teaspoon chopped sage or ¼ teaspoon dried sage	1 teaspoon chopped sage or ¼ teaspoon dried sage
2 eggs	2 eggs
50 g/2 oz soft breadcrumbs	1 cup fresh soft bread crumbs
25 g/1 oz margarine	2 tablespoons margarine
300 ml/½ pint cheese sauce (see page 29)	1¼ cups cheese sauce (see page 29)
To garnish	**To garnish**
parsley	parsley

Put the peeled onions into salted water to cover and boil steadily for 30 minutes. By this time they will not be completely cooked but it should be possible to remove the centre core. Keep the onion stock. Chop the onion cores finely, add remaining ingredients (except margarine and cheese sauce) and pile this stuffing back into the centres. Put the onions into a greased casserole. Pour over 200 ml/7 fl oz (U.S. ¾ cup) onion stock and put a small piece of margarine on each onion. Bake for 45 minutes, covered, in a moderately hot oven (190°C, 375°F, Gas Mark 5). Lift out of the stock and coat with cheese sauce. Garnish with parsley and serve hot.

Egg Dishes

Eggs are one of the most complete protein foods and can be used in a great variety of ways. If you are short of time there are few foods quicker to prepare than an egg.

Boiled eggs As well as being an excellent basis for a salad (see the illustration on page 54), soft or hard-boiled eggs can be coated with a cheese or other sauce, and served on a bed of vegetables. You will find a recipe for a cheese sauce on page 29.

Poached eggs Break the egg into boiling salted water and cook steadily for 2-3 minutes until set. Lift on to a bed of vegetables, such as creamed spinach or a purée of haricot beans, or a mixture of interesting vegetables like the Vegetable Casserole on page 74.

Omelettes, soufflés and pancakes all make excellent use of eggs, and you will find a variety of recipes in this chapter.

Savoury Panperdy

Illustrated opposite

Serves 2

Cut 3 large slices of bread into small dice, the crusts can be removed if desired. Fry in 25 g/1 oz (U.S. 2 tablespoons) hot butter until golden brown; turn once or twice then remove from the pan. Beat 4 eggs with a little seasoning, add 1 tablespoon chopped parsley and/or chopped chives. Heat another 25 g/1 oz (U.S. 2 tablespoons) butter in an omelette pan and cook the eggs as described on page 53. When the egg mixture is set spoon the fried croûtons of bread and 75 g/3 oz (U.S. ¾ cup) grated Gouda cheese over half the omelette. Fold and serve at once, garnished with more grated Gouda cheese and chopped chives.

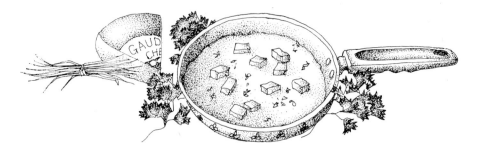

Savoury Panperdy (see above)

Making a Quiche

A quiche is a flan filled with a savoury mixture based on egg and milk or egg and cream. It is an excellent way in which to use vegetables. Cheese is often added for extra flavour and protein value.

Mushroom and Spinach Quiche

Serves 4-6

Make shortcrust pastry using 175 g/6 oz (U.S. 1½ cups) plain flour, etc. (see page 38). Roll out the pastry and line a 25-cm/10-inch shallow flan tin or ring. Place a piece of greased paper inside the pastry, with the greased side touching the dough, then crusts of bread or dried beans to weigh down the pastry (known as baking 'blind'). Cook for 10 minutes only in the centre of a moderately hot oven (200°C, 400°F, Gas Mark 6), then remove paper, etc.

Meanwhile cook approximately 225 g/8 oz (U.S. ½ lb) fresh or frozen spinach. Slice 100 g/4 oz (U.S. 1 cup) mushrooms and fry gently in 25 g/1 oz (U.S. 2 tablespoons) butter or margarine. Drain and chop or sieve the spinach, blend with the mushrooms, salt and pepper to taste, 2 large eggs, 200 ml/7½ fl oz (U.S. 1 cup) single cream and 100-175 g/4-6 oz (U.S. 1-1½ cups) grated Cheddar or Gouda cheese. Spoon into the half-baked pastry case. Return to the oven, reduce the heat to moderate (160°C, 325°F, Gas Mark 3) and cook for about 25 minutes until firm.

Freezing This, like most quiches, freezes well for 3 months.

Eggs Piquant

Serves 4

Metric·Imperial	American
1 medium onion	1 medium onion
50 g/2 oz butter or margarine	¼ cup butter or margarine
½ teaspoon made mustard	½ teaspoon made mustard
½ teaspoon curry powder	½ teaspoon curry powder
salt and pepper	salt and pepper
8 eggs, hard-boiled	8 eggs, hard-cooked
For the sauce	**For the sauce**
25 g/1 oz butter or margarine	2 tablespoons butter or margarine
25 g/1 oz flour	¼ cup all-purpose flour
½-1 teaspoon curry powder	½-1 teaspoon curry powder
300 ml/½ pint milk	1¼ cups milk
½ teaspoon made mustard	½ teaspoon made mustard
1 tablespoon mango chutney	1 tablespoon mango chutney
salt and pepper	salt and pepper
For the topping	**For the topping**
50 g/2 oz soft breadcrumbs	1 cup fresh soft bread crumbs
25 g/1 oz butter or margarine	2 tablespoons butter or margarine

Peel and finely chop the onion. Heat the butter or margarine and fry the onion, then stir in the mustard, curry powder and seasoning. Halve the eggs lengthways, chop and blend the yolks with the onion mixture. Pack into the whites and put cut side downwards in a shallow ovenproof dish.

Make a sauce of the butter, flour mixed with the curry powder, milk, mustard and chutney (see page 29), taste and season well. Pour over the eggs. Top with the crumbs and butter or margarine, in tiny pieces, and bake for approximately 15-20 minutes towards the top of a moderate oven (180°C, 350°F, Gas Mark 4).

Soufflés are an excellent way of combining the protein value of eggs with other foods in a savoury or sweet dish. The carrot soufflé, below, has a more moist texture than the classic cheese soufflé. As the amount of sauce in the carrot soufflé is high, it should therefore be baked in a slightly hotter oven.

Cheese Soufflé

Serves 3

Make a sauce (see page 29), but use only 150 ml/¼ pint (U.S. ⅔ cup) milk to the 25 g/1 oz (U.S. 2 tablespoons) butter or margarine and 25 g/1 oz (U.S. ¼ cup) flour if you want a firm texture, or increase the amount of milk by several tablespoons if you require a lighter and softer mixture. Add approximately 100 g/4 oz (U.S. 1 cup) grated cheese, seasoning to taste, then 3-4 egg yolks and finally fold in 4 stiffly whisked egg whites. Bake for 35 minutes in the centre of a moderately hot oven (190°C, 375°F, Gas Mark 5).

Variation
If you use a vegetable purée instead of the milk you produce a most deliciously flavoured dish.

Carrot Soufflé

Serves 4

Metric·Imperial	American
225 g/8 oz cooked carrots	½ lb cooked carrots
50 g/2 oz butter	¼ cup butter
50 g/2 oz flour	½ cup all-purpose flour
3 tablespoons carrot stock	4 tablespoons carrot stock
300 ml/½ pint milk	1¼ cups milk
little grated lemon rind	little grated lemon rind
cayenne pepper	cayenne pepper
¼ teaspoon grated nutmeg	¼ teaspoon grated nutmeg
4 eggs	4 eggs
little chopped parsley	little chopped parsley

Mash, sieve or liquidise the carrots until a smooth purée. Melt the butter in a saucepan and stir in the flour. Gradually add the carrot stock and milk and simmer to make a creamy sauce, stirring continually. Flavour with lemon rind, cayenne pepper and nutmeg. Add the carrot purée and blend with the sauce. Separate the eggs, adding the yolks to the carrot mixture. Whisk the egg whites until they are stiff but not too dry. Using a metal spoon, lightly fold the whites into the sauce. Butter a 1.25-litre/2-pint (U.S. 2½-pint) soufflé dish, sprinkle with chopped parsley, then put in the carrot mixture. Bake for 35 minutes in the centre of a moderately hot oven (200°C, 400°F, Gas Mark 6). Serve as soon as the soufflé is cooked.

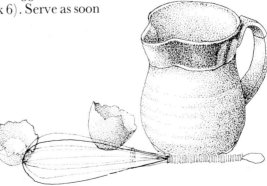

Making Batters

Sift a generous 100 g/4 oz (U.S. 1 cup) flour with a pinch of salt, add 1 egg and 300 ml/½ pint (U.S. 1¼ cups) milk or milk and water. If you use 2 eggs, then deduct 2 tablespoons (U.S. 3 tablespoons) milk or milk and water.

To make pancakes heat a little oil or fat in a pan, pour in enough of the batter to give a paper thin coating. Cook for about 2 minutes, then toss or turn and cook on the other side. Continue with the rest of the batter. This should make approximately 8 pancakes, enough for 4 portions.

Pancakes can be filled with cooked vegetables in a cheese sauce (see the recipe on page 29), with vegetable purées or with the lentil curry mixture on page 78.

Cheese Puffballs

Illustrated opposite
Makes 30 balls

Metric·Imperial	American
3 eggs	3 eggs
225 g/8 oz Cheddar cheese, finely grated	2 cups finely grated Cheddar cheese
2 tablespoons pale ale	3 tablespoons light beer
salt and pepper	salt and pepper
50 g/2 oz plain flour	½ cup all-purpose flour
1 teaspoon baking powder	1 teaspoon baking powder
30 Spanish stuffed green olives	30 Spanish stuffed green olives
For frying	**For frying**
oil	oil

Separate the eggs and put the yolks into a bowl. Mix with the cheese, ale and seasoning. Sift the flour and baking powder into the cheese mixture. Stiffly whisk the egg whites and fold into the cheese batter. Allow to stand for 30 minutes. Form into about 30 balls, with floured fingers, putting an olive in the centre of each ball. The batter should be firm enough to handle, but if necessary add a little extra flour. Fry in hot deep oil for about 2-3 minutes, until golden and puffed out. Drain on absorbent paper and serve immediately.

Cheese and Pasta Fritters

Makes 12

Metric·Imperial	American
75 g/3 oz *cooked* short cut macaroni	¾ cup *cooked* short cut macaroni
3 eggs	3 eggs
75 g/3 oz Cheddar cheese, finely grated	¾ cup finely grated Cheddar cheese
salt and pepper	salt and pepper
1 tablespoon chopped parsley	1 tablespoon chopped parsley
For frying	**For frying**
oil	oil
To garnish	**To garnish**
lettuce	lettuce

Put the macaroni into a basin, chop a little more finely with a knife and fork. Add the eggs, cheese, a little salt and pepper and the parsley. Heat a little oil in the frying pan. Drop spoonfuls of the pasta mixture into the oil. Cook steadily for approximately 1½ minutes until set and golden-brown on the underside. Turn and cook for the same time on the second side. Serve hot or cold on a bed of lettuce.

Cheese Puffballs (see above)

Devilled Eggs

Illustrated on pages 54-55
Serves 3 as a light main dish

Metric·Imperial	American
3 eggs, hard-boiled	3 eggs, hard-cooked
3 sticks celery	3 stalks celery
175 g/6 oz cream cheese	¾ cup cream cheese
½ teaspoon grated nutmeg	½ teaspoon grated nutmeg
salt and freshly ground black pepper	salt and freshly ground black pepper
To garnish	**To garnish**
1 (113-g/4-oz) jar Spanish stuffed green olives	1 (4-oz) jar Spanish stuffed green olives
For the Devilled Sauce	**For the Devilled Sauce**
1 teaspoon made mustard	1 teaspoon made mustard
2 tablespoons tomato ketchup	3 tablespoons tomato ketchup
1 lemon	1 lemon
few drops Tabasco sauce	few drops Tabasco sauce
1 teaspoon mushroom ketchup	1 teaspoon mushroom ketchup
1 tablespoon tomato chutney	1 tablespoon tomato chutney
salt and pepper	salt and pepper

Cut the hard-boiled eggs in half lengthwise and remove the yolks carefully. Reserve a little for garnish. Cut the celery into neat lengths. Stand the egg whites on a dish with the celery. Mix the egg yolks with the cream cheese, nutmeg, salt and black pepper. Combine the mixture well and pipe into the egg whites and on to the celery sticks. Garnish with some sliced stuffed green olives. Put the remaining olives in a bowl and place in the centre of the dish. Sieve the reserved egg yolks over the celery sticks.

Put the mustard and tomato ketchup into a basin, squeeze out the juice from the lemon, blend this with the rest of the ingredients for the Devilled Sauce. Trickle over the eggs; serve the remaining sauce separately.

Omelettes

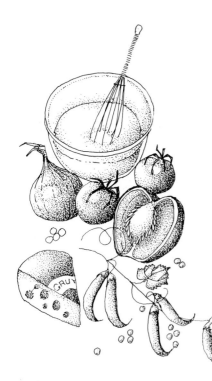

To make a perfect omelette remember: make certain the butter is really hot before you add the egg mixture. Cook the mixture quickly, working a plain omelette as the recipe.

Serve the omelette AS SOON AS IT IS COOKED.

There are three basic types of omelette:

a The plain or French type. In this the eggs are beaten only very lightly. This is generally a savoury dish.

b The Spanish type (Tortilla). This is really an extension of the plain omelette, but the egg mixture is not folded in the same way. It is a splendid way of using small quantities of mixed vegetables.

c The soufflé omelette. For this dish the eggs are separated and you have a thick 'puffy' egg mixture, which is difficult to cook entirely OVER heat, so it is completed under the grill, see details below.

Normally omelettes are cooked in a pan, but you can bake a similar mixture in the oven (see the recipe for Soufflé Omelette Espagnole, page 57).

To make an omelette for 2 people, you need from 3 eggs. This number would give you a rather small omelette, suitable for a light meal only. For a main meal allow at least 2 eggs per person.

Use the right-sized omelette pan, for example Cheese Omelette (see page 53) should be cooked in a 15-18 cm/6-7 inch pan. If the pan is too small the eggs take too long to cook and will be rather tough; if, on the other hand, the pan is too large the omelette will be thin and rather dry.

In this type of omelette it is important to half cook the egg mixture over the hotplate or gas burner, then transfer the pan to a heated grill so the mixture cooks from above. This means that the omelette does not get over-cooked, for it is impossible to 'work' a soufflé type in the same way as one does a plain omelette. Check the pan handle does not become burned with the heat of the grill.

You can fill a soufflé omelette with a savoury mixture, or with hot jam or hot fruit. To fold the cooked mixture make a slit down the centre (for the omelette should be so thick that normal folding is virtually impossible), then fold away from the handle and tip out on to the serving dish.

Soufflé Omelettes

Cheese Omelette

Serves 2-3

Metric·Imperial	American
50-100 g/2-4 oz cheese, grated	½-1 cup grated cheese
4-5 eggs	4-5 eggs
salt and pepper	salt and pepper
little water	little water
25-40 g/1-1½ oz butter	2-3 tablespoons butter
To garnish	**To garnish**
little parsley or watercress	little parsley or watercress

It is imperative to grate the cheese before making the omelette so the eggs are not overcooked by being kept waiting. Break the eggs into a basin, add seasoning and a little water. I generally allow half an egg shell of water to each egg, but this is purely a matter of taste (water gives a lighter omelette).

Heat the butter in the pan, pour in the eggs. DO NOTHING for half a minute, to allow the eggs to set lightly at the bottom. With a fork or palette knife push the eggs from the sides of the pan and tilt the pan, so the liquid egg runs down. This makes sure the omelette cooks evenly and quickly. Continue 'working' the omelette in this way until nearly set. Add most of the cheese, heat for half a minute, roll or fold away from the handle. Tip on to a hot dish, top with the rest of the cheese, garnish and serve.

Variations
If preferred, you can add all the cheese to the eggs before cooking, this gives a drier textured omelette. Slimmers could use cottage cheese as a filling in the omelette; but do not mix the cottage cheese with the uncooked eggs.

Fillings for omelettes
Mushrooms or other vegetables can be cooked and put into the omelette before folding or rolling; chopped fried mushrooms can be added to the eggs before cooking. Some of the best fillings are: asparagus, artichoke hearts (as illustrated on page 58) or diced mixed root vegetables, in a white, cheese or parsley sauce or just tossed in hot butter.

Rice: Cooked brown or white rice, blended with a little hot margarine, chopped chives, parsley and grated cheese makes a sustaining filling.

Herbs make an excellent flavouring. Use just a pinch of dried herbs or 1-2 teaspoons of freshly chopped herbs to the amount of eggs above. Parsley, chives, sage (use sparingly), thyme (use sparingly) and fennel are some of the best herbs to use.

Overleaf: Devilled Eggs (see page 52)

Bean Sprout Omelette

Serves 3-4

Metric·Imperial	American
100-150 g/4-5 oz fresh or canned bean sprouts	2-2½ cups fresh or canned bean sprouts
3 tablespoons finely diced red pepper	4 tablespoons finely diced red pepper
6 eggs	6 eggs
salt and pepper	salt and pepper
2 tablespoons single cream	3 tablespoons light cream
50 g/2 oz butter	¼ cup butter
For the topping	**For the topping**
2-3 tablespoons double cream	3-4 tablespoons heavy cream
50 g/2 oz Gruyère cheese, grated	½ cup grated Gruyère cheese

If using fresh bean sprouts, cook for 1-2 minutes only, or heat canned bean sprouts for just 1 minute. It is essential they remain crisp. Drain well. Blend the bean sprouts and red pepper with the eggs, seasoning and single cream. Heat the butter in a large omelette pan and cook the mixture until lightly set, fold and slide on to a hot flameproof dish. Spread the omelette with the double cream. Top with the grated Gruyère cheese and heat for 1-2 minutes under a hot grill.

Spanish Omelette (Tortilla)

Serves 3-4

Metric·Imperial	American
1-2 onions	1-2 onions
3 medium potatoes, cooked	3 medium potatoes, cooked
½-1 red pepper (canned or fresh)	½-1 red pepper (canned or fresh)
2 tablespoons oil	3 tablespoons oil
few cooked peas	few cooked peas
6 eggs	6 eggs
salt and pepper	salt and pepper
little water	little water
50 g/2 oz butter	¼ cup butter

Peel and chop the onions, dice the potatoes, dice the pepper (discard the core and seeds from a fresh pepper). Heat the oil in a large omelette pan, toss the onion in this for 1-2 minutes, add the potatoes, peas and pepper. Cook until the onion is tender and the rest of the ingredients hot. Beat the eggs in a basin, add the seasoning and a little water, then mix in the hot vegetables. Heat the butter in the omelette pan and cook as for a plain omelette (see page 53) but do not fold or roll. Slide on to a hot dish and cut into 4 portions. Serve hot, although in Spain slices of this tortilla are often eaten as a cold picnic dish.

Note If you do not want to use oil in cooking the vegetables, or if you are using raw potatoes, then dice and simmer in salted water or stock first, until tender, then drain and use as above.

Freezing Do not freeze this omelette although it is an excellent idea to freeze small quantities of prepared vegetables

Metric·Imperial	American
1 onion	1 onion
2-3 tomatoes	2-3 tomatoes
1 green pepper	1 green pepper
few mushrooms	few mushrooms
little oil	little oil
2 tablespoons stock	3 tablespoons stock
salt and pepper	salt and pepper
100 g/4 oz cooked potato or other vegetable	$\frac{1}{4}$ lb cooked potato or other vegetable
50 g/2 oz butter	$\frac{1}{4}$ cup butter
5-6 eggs	5-6 eggs
2 tablespoons milk	3 tablespoons milk

Soufflé Omelette Espagnole

Serves 3-4

Peel and chop the onion, skin and slice the tomatoes, chop the green pepper (discarding core and seeds) and chop the mushrooms. Heat the oil in a pan and fry the vegetables for a few minutes. Add the stock so the mixture is kept hot and moist. Season well. Dice the potato and add to the other vegetables.

Put the butter into a large, shallow ovenproof dish; heat in the oven for a few minutes. Separate the eggs. Beat the egg yolks with milk and seasoning, whisk the egg whites and fold into the yolks. Remove the dish from the oven and pour in the omelette mixture. Bake for about 15 minutes above the centre of a hot oven (220°C, 425°F, Gas Mark 7) until lightly set. Slip the omelette out of the dish, or serve in this, topped with the hot vegetable mixture.

Pasta and Rice

Both these foods provide an excellent basis for vegetarian dishes. It is, however, essential that they are correctly cooked, to retain their flavour and texture.

There are a great variety of pasta shapes, also a choice of wholemeal and white pasta; this means you can choose the type of pasta you prefer and the best shape for a particular dish. As pasta is made from flour it is a source of protein and the important B group of vitamins.

Always make certain the liquid is boiling before adding the pasta to the pan and use an adequate amount of liquid. This makes sure the pasta does not stick, either to the pan or to itself.

There is an interesting point about cooking thin strips of pasta noodles or cannelloni (the large tubes of pasta used in the recipe overleaf). If you prepare the dish for freezing there is no need to pre-cook the pasta, for it softens during the process of freezing and cooking when defrosted. Many people now like to use this technique; personally I find that although it saves the boiling process first you do need to cook the complete dish rather longer in the oven which tends to dry out the sauces. It is however a matter of personal taste. If you decide to try this technique, then allow about twice the cooking time in the oven as given in the recipes and be a little more generous with the amount of sauce.

When using rice choose the right kind for that particular dish. While a round grain rice is suitable for sweet milk puddings it is important to use a long grain for savoury dishes, to prevent it becoming sticky in cooking. You may prefer to buy brown rice, which retains more of the natural texture of the grain. Rice provides a certain amount of protein, calcium, iron and B group vitamins.

If you are cooking long grain rice to serve with a dish you require twice the volume of the liquid to rice, i.e. to 1 cup of rice use 2 cups of water. Put the rice, the cold water and a little salt into the pan. Bring gently to the boil and simmer for 15 minutes, by which time the rice should be tender but not overcooked, and the liquid absorbed. Brown and 'par-boiled' rice takes slightly longer to cook so use $2\frac{1}{2}$ cups water to each 1 cup rice.

Both rice and pasta can be used in cold, as well as hot dishes. Mix with the dressing while warm, so the flavours blend.

Artichoke Omelette (see page 53)

Quick Ways with Pasta and Rice

Top with melted butter or margarine and herbs and serve as an accompaniment to main dishes.

Mix the pasta or rice with plenty of grated cheese, chopped nuts and fresh tomato purée.

Add a little chopped cooked pasta or rice to eggs and use for omelettes or scrambled eggs, adding grated cheese or chopped herbs.

Freezing Do not store pasta or rice for too long a period, otherwise the texture is lost. See under the recipes for timing. If you break up the rice mixture with a fork when lightly frozen it is easier to reheat the mixture, as it has not formed a solid block.

Cannelloni with Olives

Serves 3 as a main dish or
5-6 as a meal starter

Metric·Imperial	**American**
5 or 6 cannelloni rolls	5 or 6 cannelloni rolls
1 (425-g/15-oz) can soya mince	1 (15-oz) can soya mince
1 tablespoon tomato purée	1 tablespoon tomato paste
1 teaspoon chopped fresh or ¼ teaspoon dried mixed herbs	1 teaspoon chopped fresh or ¼ teaspoon dried mixed herbs
1 teaspoon sugar	1 teaspoon sugar
8 Spanish stuffed green olives	8 Spanish stuffed green olives
300 ml/½ pint cheese sauce (see page 29)	1¼ cups cheese sauce (see page 29)
little extra grated cheese	little extra grated cheese
To garnish	**To garnish**
tomatoes	tomatoes

Cook the pasta in boiling salted water until just tender – drain. Put the soya mince, tomato purée, herbs and sugar in a bowl. Slice the olives and mix most of these with the other ingredients. Using a teaspoon or a piping bag with a plain nozzle, fill the pasta rolls. Place in an ovenproof dish. Pour the cheese sauce over the pasta rolls and sprinkle with cheese. Bake in the centre of a moderate oven (180°C, 350°F, Gas Mark 4) for about 20 minutes. Arrange sliced tomatoes on top and sliced olives.

Freezing Prepare the dish and freeze *without* cooking the pasta, then cook for 45 minutes. Use within 3 months.

Variation
Make double the amount of cheese sauce; mix half with 225 g/8 oz (U.S. generous 1 cup) cooked and finely chopped or sieved spinach. Use as a filling in the cannelloni.

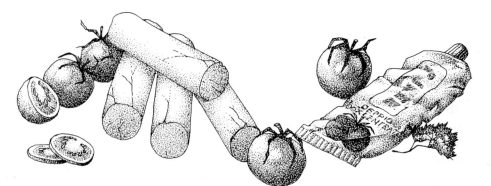

This popular pasta dish is often badly made. The secret is to use enough sauce and make sure the macaroni is not over-boiled.

Cook approximately 75 g/3 oz (U.S. ¾ cup) macaroni in boiling salted water until just soft, then drain. Make at least 300 ml/½ pint (U.S. 1¼ cups) cheese sauce (see page 29). Mix the macaroni with the sauce. If both pasta and sauce are hot, turn into a flameproof dish, top with grated cheese and soft breadcrumbs and brown under the grill. If more convenient cook for 30 minutes in the centre of a moderately hot oven (190°C, 375°F, Gas Mark 5).

Metric·Imperial	American
175 g/6 oz macaroni	1½ cups macaroni
salt and pepper	salt and pepper
4-6 eggs, hard-boiled	4-6 eggs, hard-cooked
50 g/2 oz butter or margarine	¼ cup butter or margarine
2 medium onions, chopped	2 medium onions, chopped
40 g/1½ oz flour	¼ cup plus 2 tablespoons all-purpose flour
450 ml/¾ pint milk	2 cups milk
For the topping	**For the topping**
4 medium tomatoes	4 medium tomatoes
25 g/1 oz butter or margarine	2 tablespoons butter or margarine
50 g/2 oz Cheddar cheese, grated	½ cup grated Cheddar cheese
To garnish	**To garnish**
little chopped parsley	little chopped parsley

Cook the macaroni in well seasoned boiling water until just tender, then drain. Shell and halve the eggs. Heat the butter or margarine in a pan and fry the onions until just soft, stir in the flour and then the milk. Bring to the boil, stir until a coating consistency. Mix with the macaroni and season to taste. Spoon half the macaroni mixture into an ovenproof dish, top with the halved eggs, then the rest of the macaroni mixture. Skin the tomatoes and chop fairly finely. Heat the butter or margarine and cook the tomatoes for a few minutes. Spread over the macaroni mixture, then top with the cheese and heat in the centre of a moderately hot oven (190°C, 375°F, Gas Mark 5) for about 25 minutes. Sprinkle with parsley.

Variation

Omit the tomato topping and use more grated cheese.

One of the most popular ways to serve spaghetti or any pasta is with a topping of tomato sauce and grated cheese.

Peel and finely chop 1 large onion and 1-2 cloves garlic. Skin and slice 675 g/ 1½ lb (U.S. 1½ lb) tomatoes. Heat 2 tablespoons (U.S. 3 tablespoons) oil in a saucepan. Toss the onion and garlic in the oil for 5 minutes; take care the vegetables do not brown. Add the tomatoes plus 300 ml/½ pint (U.S. 1¼ cups) water, a little sea salt, paprika and a pinch of cayenne pepper. Simmer until the tomatoes form a fairly smooth thick purée, but do not overcook. You can add 1-2 tablespoons chopped parsley and 1-2 teaspoons chopped borage if desired.

Vegetable Risotto

Serves 4-6

Metric · Imperial	American
2 medium onions	2 medium onions
2 cloves garlic (optional)	2 cloves garlic (optional)
75 g/3 oz butter or margarine	¼ cup plus 2 tablespoons butter or margarine
100 g/4 oz button mushrooms	1 cup button mushrooms
225 g/8 oz long grain rice	1 cup long grain rice
600 ml/1 pint water	2½ cups water
pinch saffron powder	pinch saffron powder
salt and pepper	salt and pepper
175 g/6 oz fresh or frozen peas	generous 1 cup fresh or frozen peas
1 green pepper	1 green pepper
3 medium tomatoes	3 medium tomatoes
50 g/2 oz pine nuts or blanched almonds	⅓ cup pine nuts or blanched almonds
100 g/4 oz Cheddar cheese, grated	1 cup grated Cheddar cheese
2 tablespoons chopped parsley	3 tablespoons chopped parsley

Peel and chop the onions and garlic. Heat the butter or margarine in a large saucepan, add the onions, garlic and mushrooms. Fry gently for a few minutes, then lift out the mushrooms and put on one side; this makes sure they do not become overcooked and also change the colour of the rice mixture. Stir the rice into the onions and garlic.

Mix the water with the saffron powder, pour into the pan, bring to the boil, stir briskly with a fork; cover the pan and simmer gently for about 10 minutes. Remove the lid, add seasoning, the peas, green pepper, cut into neat strips, and the neatly diced tomatoes. Continue cooking for another 5 minutes, then add half the nuts, cheese and parsley with the cooked mushrooms and cook for a further 2-3 minutes. Pile on to a hot dish and top with the remaining nuts, cheese and parsley.

Freezing Use within 2 months.

Variations
Use other vegetables in season; omit the saffron powder.

Egg and vegetable risotto Omit the cheese. Beat 2-3 eggs, stir into the rice mixture 2-3 minutes before the end of the cooking time. Stir as the eggs set.

Egg and Saffron Risotto

Follow the Vegetable Risotto recipe, substituting red for green peppers, and sliced hard-boiled eggs, black and green stuffed olives and drained canned artichoke hearts for the mushrooms, peas, nuts and cheese. Add the olives and artichoke hearts 5 minutes before serving to allow them to heat through.

Gourmet Coleslaw (see page 68)

Stuffed Tomatoes

Serves 4

Large firm tomatoes can be stuffed in the same way as aubergines. Cut a slice from 8 large tomatoes, scoop out the centre pulp, chop and fry with the onions, then proceed as the recipe above but bake for 15 minutes only.

Stuffed Aubergines

Serves 4

Metric·Imperial	American
4 medium aubergines	4 medium eggplants
salt and pepper	salt and pepper
2 medium onions	2 medium onions
4 large tomatoes	4 large tomatoes
50 g/2 oz butter or margarine	¼ cup butter or margarine
75 g/3 oz cooked rice	good ½ cup cooked rice
2 tablespoons chopped parsley	3 tablespoons chopped parsley
2 teaspoons lemon juice	2 teaspoons lemon juice
1 teaspoon grated lemon rind	1 teaspoon grated lemon rind
175 g/6 oz Gruyère, Gouda or Cheddar cheese, grated	1½ cups grated Gruyère, Gouda or Cheddar cheese
To garnish	**To garnish**
1-2 lemons	1-2 lemons
parsley	parsley

Halve each aubergine lengthways. Cut out the centre pulp, being careful to leave the vegetable skins intact. Sprinkle the flesh and skins lightly with salt, then leave for 30 minutes. This prevents the aubergines being bitter. Pour away any liquid. Rinse the aubergines in cold water and dry well on absorbent paper. Dice the centre pulp finely. Peel and finely chop the onions, skin and slice the tomatoes. Heat the butter or margarine in a saucepan, fry the aubergine pulp and onions until soft, add half the tomato slices, the rice, parsley, lemon juice, rind and half the cheese. Season the mixture well then spoon into the 8 aubergine halves. Put into a greased ovenproof dish, top the filling with the remainder of the tomato slices and cheese. Cover the dish and bake for 25-30 minutes in the centre of a moderate oven (180°C, 350°F, Gas Mark 4). Cut the lemon(s) into thin slices, place on each halved aubergine and top with sprigs of parsley; serve hot. Either a Cheese Sauce (see page 29), or Tomato Sauce (see page 61), would be an excellent accompaniment.

Variation
Fresh red or green peppers could be stuffed in the same way. Halve the peppers, remove the cores and seeds. Blanch for 4 minutes in boiling salted water, drain, then fill with the stuffing and bake as the recipe above.

Freezing The stuffed vegetables freeze well for 3 months.

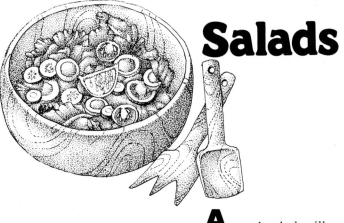

Salads

A good salad will combine a variety of interesting textures, foods and colours, to produce eye appeal as well as a good taste.

Add nuts, cheese of all kinds, eggs and some of the cooked pulses to a salad, to turn it into a main dish. The pâtés on pages 12-13 can also be served with salad to make a light supper or luncheon meal.

Seasonal fruits combine well with the more traditional salad ingredients, particularly apples, avocados (a source of protein), bananas, oranges, peaches and the berry fruits.

It is important that all green salad ingredients should look crisp and fresh, so buy wisely and store in a covered container in the refrigerator.

Cheese and Olive Salad

Illustrated on page 66
Serves 4

Dice approximately 175 g/6 oz (U.S. 1 cup) Danish Blue and the same amount of Cheddar or Gouda cheese. Cut a small fresh red and a small green pepper into narrow strips, discard the cores and seeds. Slice several tomatoes and place on a bed of cos lettuce. Pile the cheeses, pepper and several tablespoons Spanish stuffed olives on to the tomatoes.

Blend 300 ml/½ pint (U.S. 1¼ cups) natural yogurt, ¼ peeled and diced cucumber, salt, pepper, pinch cayenne pepper, 1 tablespoon lemon juice. Serve in a sauceboat.

Variation
The dressing is made more interesting by adding a little chopped mint and chives or 2-3 tablespoons (U.S. 3-4 tablespoons) salted peanuts.

Egg and Sprout Salad

Serves 4

Lightly cook 450 g/1 lb (U.S. 1 lb) tiny firm Brussels sprouts, until just tender. Drain and cool; blend with mayonnaise. Add 50 g/2 oz (U.S. ⅓ cup) sliced stuffed olives, 50 g/2 oz (U.S. ½ cup) flaked almonds, 2 chopped hard-boiled eggs. Add a little lemon juice to sharpen the dressing. Spoon on to a bed of shredded lettuce. Garnish with sliced hard-boiled eggs and flaked almonds.

Overleaf left: Cheese and Olive Salad (see above)
Overleaf right: Summer-time Pie (see page 36)

Piperade Salad

Serves 4

Metric·Imperial	American
1 large onion	1 large onion
1 clove garlic	1 clove garlic
1 red pepper	1 red pepper
3 large tomatoes	3 large tomatoes
50 g/2 oz butter or margarine	$\frac{1}{4}$ cup butter or margarine
6 eggs	6 eggs
4 tablespoons mayonnaise	5 tablespoons mayonnaise
salt and pepper	salt and pepper
lettuce, watercress	lettuce, watercress
$\frac{1}{4}$ cucumber	$\frac{1}{4}$ cucumber
For the vinaigrette dressing	**For the vinaigrette dressing**
$\frac{1}{2}$ teaspoon made mustard	$\frac{1}{2}$ teaspoon made mustard
pinch salt	pinch salt
freshly ground black pepper	freshly ground black pepper
pinch sugar	pinch sugar
5 tablespoons salad oil	6 tablespoons salad oil
3 tablespoons white wine vinegar or lemon juice	$\frac{1}{4}$ cup white wine vinegar or lemon juice

Peel and finely chop the onion and garlic; dice the pepper, discard the core and seeds; skin and dice the tomatoes. Heat the butter or margarine and cook the vegetables until soft. Beat the eggs, add to the hot vegetable mixture and scramble lightly. Add the mayonnaise, salt and pepper to taste. Allow to cool.

Shred the lettuce, sprig the watercress, slice the cucumber. Put into a salad bowl. Blend the mustard, salt, pepper and sugar with the oil and vinegar or lemon juice. Spoon a little over the salad. Top with the creamy Piperade.

Gourmet Coleslaw

Illustrated on page 63
Serves 4-6

Metric·Imperial	American
1 head Chinese leaves (Chinese cabbage)	1 head Chinese leaves (Chinese cabbage)
1 small head celery	1 small bunch celery
1 green pepper	1 green pepper
1 red pepper	1 red pepper
1 medium onion	1 medium onion
2 eggs, hard-boiled	2 eggs, hard-cooked
few slices avocado (dipped in lemon juice)	few slices avocado (dipped in lemon juice)
mayonnaise	mayonnaise

Wash, dry and shred some of the Chinese leaves and celery. Any left keeps well if lightly wrapped in polythene and stored in the refrigerator or a cool place. Cut the peppers into rings, discard the core and seeds. Peel and slice the onion. Mix all these ingredients together. Top with the halved or quartered eggs, avocado slices and chopped celery, and serve with mayonnaise.

Variation
Toss the salad in an oil and vinegar dressing.

Pasta Slaw

Serves 4-6

Metric·Imperial	American
75 g/3 oz pasta	¾ cup pasta
salt and pepper	salt and pepper
225 g/8 oz fresh or frozen French beans	½ lb fresh or frozen French beans
1 small green pepper	1 small green pepper
1 medium carrot	1 medium carrot
4 spring onions	4 scallions
75 g/3 oz white cabbage, shredded	1 cup shredded white cabbage
4 tablespoons mayonnaise	⅓ cup mayonnaise
2 tablespoons milk or single cream	3 tablespoons milk or light cream
1 tablespoon vinegar	1 tablespoon vinegar
2 teaspoons sugar	2 teaspoons sugar

You can choose any pasta shapes for the dish, but the smaller type, i.e. shells, rings, spirals, are the most suitable. Cook the pasta in well seasoned boiling water until just tender, then strain and rinse under cold water. Meanwhile cook and strain the beans; allow to cool. Dice the pepper, discarding core and seeds. Peel and grate the carrot, chop the onions. Mix all the ingredients together.

Variation

Use cooked brown rice instead of pasta.

Savoury Cheese Log

Serves 4-6

Metric·Imperial	American
4 eggs, hard-boiled	4 eggs, hard-cooked
225 g/8 oz Cheddar cheese, grated	2 cups grated Cheddar cheese
6-8 stuffed olives	6-8 stuffed olives
6-8 gherkins	6-8 sweet dill pickles
2 tablespoons chopped chives or spring onions	3 tablespoons chopped chives or scallions
1 teaspoon made mustard	1 teaspoon made mustard
2 tablespoons mayonnaise	3 tablespoons mayonnaise
2 tablespoons single cream	3 tablespoons light cream
salt and pepper	salt and pepper
To garnish	**To garnish**
3-4 olives	3-4 olives
1 tomato	1 tomato
1 gherkin	1 sweet dill pickle

Shell and chop the eggs. Put the grated cheese in a bowl. Slice the olives and gherkins; mix the chopped eggs, olives, gherkins and chives with the cheese. Stir in the mustard, mayonnaise and cream, taste the mixture and season very well. Form into a roll with damp hands, wrap in aluminium foil and leave in the refrigerator for about 1 hour to chill. Unwrap and put on to a dish. Garnish with a design of olives, a tomato cut into 'petals' and a gherkin cut into the shape of leaves. Serve with a salad.

Overleaf left: Chestnut Croquettes (see page 73)
Overleaf right: Avocado Pâté (see page 13)

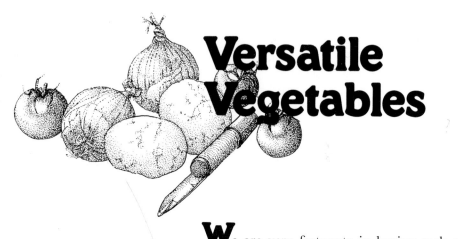

Versatile Vegetables

We are very fortunate in having such a wide variety of vegetables available, and excellent dishes and meals can be prepared, using vegetables as the basic ingredient, rather than as an accompaniment to other foods. If you are preparing vegetable dishes then make sure that you have incorporated sufficient protein. Obviously the dish must be considered in relation to other meals served during the day.

There are many simple ways of adding protein to a vegetable dish: you can incorporate nuts, as shown in the recipe below and the picture on page 19, you can mix green or root vegetables with the pulses (beans, lentils and peas), and you can incorporate eggs, cheese or pasta (for flour has some protein value).

There are now on the market a selection of products based upon textured vegetable protein (T.V.P.) These vary, some are in dried form, others are meant to be extenders to meat. Another type is as soya chunks or mince, sold in cans. In some cases these soya products are flavoured with meat gravy, so you should always check the ingredients before purchasing. The canned product just needs reheating, although most people prefer to combine it with other ingredients to give additional flavour. Ways of using T.V.P. are on page 41. Soya beans, upon which all these T.V.P. products are based, are a highly nutritious form of protein.

Vegetables with Savoury Butters

Cooked fresh, frozen or canned vegetables can be turned into a more interesting and sustaining dish if topped with savoury butters. Here are some flavours you can make:

Almond and Lemon Butter

Grate the rind from 1 lemon; squeeze out 1 tablespoon juice. Blend with 50 g/2 oz (U.S. ¼ cup) butter and 50 g/2 oz (U.S. good ½ cup) blanched or unblanched chopped almonds. Other nuts can be used in place of the almonds.

Garlic Butter

Peel and crush 2 cloves of garlic with a pinch of salt, beat into 50 g/2 oz (U.S. ¼ cup) butter, then add pepper and salt to taste.

Gherkin Butter

Blend ½-1 teaspoon made mustard with 50 g/2 oz (U.S. ¼ cup) butter, then add 3-4 finely chopped cocktail gherkins and a pinch of black or cayenne pepper.

Herb Butter

Cream 50 g/2 oz (U.S. ¼ cup) butter with 1 teaspoon lemon juice, then add various herbs, e.g. 2 tablespoons (U.S. 3 tablespoons) chopped chives or parsley or fresh mixed herbs. Add seasoning to taste.

Nuts add Food Value

Nuts of all kinds add important food value to vegetables. An interesting and appetising way to serve fresh or frozen Brussels sprouts is to cook them in boiling water until just tender then strain. Meanwhile toss blanched flaked or coarsely chopped almonds in a little hot butter or margarine, season with freshly ground black pepper and spoon over the sprouts just before serving.

Cauliflower and broccoli spears can be topped in the same way.

Chestnut Croquettes

Illustrated on page 70
Serves 4-6

Metric·Imperial	American
450 g/1 lb chestnuts	1 lb chestnuts
water to cover	water to cover
50 g/2 oz soft breadcrumbs	1 cup fresh soft bread crumbs
2 tablespoons finely chopped celery	3 tablespoons finely chopped celery
seasoning	seasoning
1 egg	1 egg
little milk	little milk
300 ml/½ pint cheese sauce (see page 29)	1¼ cups cheese sauce (see page 29)

Slit the chestnuts, boil in water for nearly 10 minutes, drain then skin while warm. Put the shelled nuts into fresh water and simmer a further 15 minutes until soft enough to rub through a sieve or liquidise. Mix the nut purée, breadcrumbs, celery, seasoning, beaten egg and just enough milk to bind. Form into croquettes and place in an ovenproof casserole. Pour the hot sauce over the croquettes. Bake for about 15 minutes in the centre of a hot oven (220°C, 425°F, Gas Mark 7).

Freezing Open-freeze, then wrap. Use within 1 month.

Variations

Coat the croquettes in beaten egg and crumbs. Fry in hot oil then drain on absorbent paper and serve with the cheese sauce.

Use a mixture of nuts instead of chestnuts. Put through a mincer or blend in a liquidiser to produce a smooth purée.

Bean croquettes Soak overnight and then cook 175 g/6 oz (U.S. scant 1 cup) haricot beans until tender, and proceed as for chestnut croquettes.

Flakie

Serves 4-6

Metric · Imperial	American
450 g/1 lb French or other green beans	1 lb green beans
salt and pepper	salt and pepper
2 medium onions	2 medium onions
450 g/1 lb tomatoes	1 lb tomatoes
2 tablespoons oil	3 tablespoons oil
To garnish	**To garnish**
chopped parsley	chopped parsley
chopped chives	chopped chives

Prepare the beans and cook for 10 minutes only in seasoned boiling water, strain and reserve 150 ml/$\frac{1}{4}$ pint (U.S. $\frac{2}{3}$ cup) of the liquid. Meanwhile, peel and slice the onions and tomatoes very thinly. Toss for 10 minutes in the hot oil until a fairly soft purée. Add the beans and liquid, together with a little more seasoning. Cook steadily, with the lid off the pan, until the excess liquid has been evaporated and the beans are tender. Garnish with parsley and chives. Serve hot or cold as a vegetable dish or a starter.

Freezing This dish is better eaten when freshly cooked, but it is a good way to use frozen beans.

Variation
Add 1-2 chopped cloves garlic to the onion and tomatoes. Flavour with chopped basil and a little lemon juice.

Vegetable Casserole

Illustrated opposite
Serves 6-8 as a starter and 4 as a vegetable dish

Metric · Imperial	American
2 medium aubergines	2 medium eggplants
salt and pepper	salt and pepper
1 large onion	1 large onion
1-2 cloves garlic	1-2 cloves garlic
1 green or yellow pepper	1 green or yellow pepper
1 red pepper	1 red pepper
4 courgettes	4 zucchini
6 large tomatoes	6 large tomatoes
6 tablespoons oil	$\frac{1}{2}$ cup oil
2 tablespoons chopped parsley	3 tablespoons chopped parsley

Wipe the aubergines and slice thickly. Sprinkle with a little salt and leave for 15-30 minutes. The salt draws out the rather bitter taste from the aubergines. Drain off the liquid (you can rinse the aubergine slices if you do not require much salt in the recipe). Peel and chop the onion and garlic. Dice the peppers, discarding core and seeds. Wipe and slice the courgettes; do not use the rather tough ends. Skin and slice the tomatoes.

Heat the oil in a pan and add the onion, garlic and tomatoes. Cook gently for a few minutes until the tomato juice begins to flow then add the remaining vegetables. Cover and simmer gently for 35-40 minutes. Do not overcook as the vegetables should retain much of their texture. Season to taste and add the parsley towards the end of the cooking period. Serve hot or cold, garnished with a little more chopped parsley.

Freezing This freezes well. Use within 1 year.

Variation
Ratatouille Use the recipe above but cook rather longer until you have a softer texture.

Vegetable Casserole (see above)

Lentil Rissoles with Tomato Sauce

Serves 4 as a main course, 8 as a starter

Metric·Imperial	American
100 g/4 oz lentils	½ cup lentils
salt and pepper	salt and pepper
1 onion	1 onion
25 g/1 oz bran buds	1 cup bran buds
50 g/2 oz soft breadcrumbs	1 cup fresh soft bread crumbs
1 tablespoon tomato purée	1 tablespoon tomato paste
1 teaspoon chopped sage	1 teaspoon chopped sage
1 egg	1 egg
To coat	**To coat**
1 egg	1 egg
50 g/2 oz dried breadcrumbs	½ cup dry bread crumbs
For the sauce	**For the sauce**
1 onion	1 onion
2 tablespoons oil	3 tablespoons oil
15 g/½ oz flour	2 tablespoons all-purpose flour
300 ml/½ pint lentil stock	1¼ cups lentil stock
1 (227-g/8-oz) can tomatoes	1 (8-oz) can tomatoes
1 tablespoon tomato ketchup	1 tablespoon tomato ketchup
salt and pepper	salt and pepper
For frying	**For frying**
oil	oil

Soak the lentils overnight, cook in seasoned water for 1 hour or until tender. Drain but save some of the stock for the sauce. Peel and chop or grate the onion, mix with the lentils, bran buds, breadcrumbs, tomato purée, seasoning, sage and egg. Allow to stand for about 30 minutes to stiffen, shape into 8 balls. Beat the egg, coat the rissoles in egg and crumbs, leave again for a short time in a cold place to become quite firm.

Meanwhile, make the sauce. Peel and chop or grate the onion, fry in the oil for several minutes, add the flour, then the lentil stock, tomatoes and liquid from the can. Return to the heat, bring to the boil, stirring well. Add the tomato ketchup and seasoning to taste. Simmer gently until a thick purée. Sieve or blend in the liquidiser if a smooth sauce is required. Meanwhile, fry the rissoles in hot oil, drain on absorbent paper and serve with the sauce.

Freezing Open freeze then wrap; use within 2 months. Fry or reheat from the frozen state.

Variation
Bean rissoles Use haricot beans in place of lentils. Soak, then cook until tender. If using canned beans allow about 350 g/12 oz (U.S. ¾ lb).

Peanut Bake

Serves 4-5

Mince, chop or liquidise 225 g/8 oz (U.S. generous 1 cup) shelled peanuts. Mix 75 g/3 oz (U.S. 6 tablespoons) margarine or peanut butter with 75 g/3 oz (U.S. 1½ cups) soft wholemeal breadcrumbs. Skin and chop 4 tomatoes and mix with ¼ teaspoon chopped sage, ½ teaspoon chopped thyme, a pinch of salt and a pinch of cayenne pepper. Put half the crumb mixture at the bottom of a shallow ovenproof dish. Add the peanuts to the tomato mixture, spread over the crumbs, then top with the remaining crumb mixture. Bake in the centre of a moderately hot oven (200°C, 400°F, Gas Mark 6) for 25-40 minutes. Serve hot with salad.

Onion Parcels

Serves 4

Metric·Imperial	American
225 g/8 oz frozen chopped spinach	½ lb frozen chopped spinach
4 large onions	4 large onions
salt and pepper	salt and pepper
25 g/1 oz bran buds	1 cup bran buds
2 eggs, hard-boiled	2 eggs, hard-cooked
For the pastry	**For the basic pie dough**
225 g/8 oz plain flour	2 cups all-purpose flour
salt and pepper	salt and pepper
100 g/4 oz margarine or	½ cup margarine or
vegetarian fat	vegetarian shortening
little water	little water
To glaze	**To glaze**
little milk	little milk

Defrost and drain the spinach but do not cook. Peel the onions and par-boil in a little seasoned water for 10 minutes. Drain and cool. Scoop out the centres of the whole onions with a small spoon. Mix the spinach, bran buds, chopped eggs and seasoning together, fill onions with this.

Make the pastry. Sift the flour and seasoning together, rub in the fat then bind with cold water. Roll out and cut into four 15-cm/6-inch squares. Place the onions in the centre of the pastry. Moisten the edges and bring the four corners to the top of onion – seal all the edges well and flute the pastry to decorate. Place on a baking tray. Brush with a little milk and bake in a moderate oven (180°C, 350°F, Gas Mark 4) for 45 minutes. Serve hot.

Freezing These freeze well for 3 months after cooking or for 2 months if prepared, then frozen. Defrost before reheating or cooking. Freezing does mean however you cannot use hard-boiled eggs; use beaten eggs and slightly more bran buds to stiffen the mixture.

Celery with Mushrooms and Cream

Illustrated on page 79
Serves 4

Clean and chop 1 medium head of celery and place in an ovenproof dish with a little vegetable stock or wine. Dot with butter or margarine, season with salt and freshly ground pepper, cover with foil and cook in a moderate oven (180°C, 350°F, Gas Mark 4) for 20 minutes. Meanwhile slice and fry 100 g/ 4 oz (U.S. 1 cup) mushrooms in butter or margarine. Scatter mushrooms over the braised celery, pour over 150 ml/¼ pint (U.S. ⅔ cup) soured cream, sprinkle with 50 g/2 oz (U.S. ½ cup) grated cheese and return to the oven to heat through. Serve as a vegetable dish or a starter.

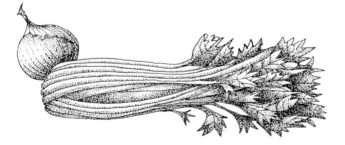

Making a Curry

There is something very warming and satisfying about a curry and the recipe below makes use of an important and relatively inexpensive protein food. To make a change add cooked vegetables (beans are especially good) with a little liquid curry mixture, instead of lentils. You could prepare the curry mixture, add enough liquid (milk or water) to make a sauce, then heat shelled hard-boiled eggs in this.

Lentil Curry

Serves 4

Metric·Imperial	American
225 g/8 oz lentils	1 cup lentils•
salt and pepper	salt and pepper
2 large onions	2 large onions
1 small apple	1 small apple
50 g/2 oz margarine or vegetarian fat	$\frac{1}{4}$ cup margarine or vegetarian shortening
1 tablespoon curry powder	1 tablespoon curry powder
1 teaspoon sugar	1 teaspoon sugar
2 teaspoons chutney	2 teaspoons chutney
few drops lemon juice	few drops lemon juice
To serve	**To serve**
boiled rice	boiled rice

Soak the lentils in water to cover for a few hours, then simmer in the same water for approximately 40 minutes until just soft, keeping the lentils whole. Season well.

Peel and chop the onions and apple and fry in the fat until soft. Add the curry powder towards the end of the cooking period. Mix in the lentils with any liquid in the pan and all the other ingredients. Heat well, then spoon over the boiled rice

To serve with curries
Sliced bananas, dipped in lemon juice; sliced red and green peppers, mixed with sliced onions and tomatoes; nuts, various, freshly grated coconut; poppadums; sliced cucumber in natural yogurt; various chutneys.

Variations
Add 1-2 tablespoons desiccated coconut and 1-2 tablespoons sultanas to the lentils and other ingredients.

Serve as a cold curry topped with yogurt and thinly sliced cucumber. Omit the rice and garnish with watercress, sliced tomatoes, spring onions and rings of green pepper.

Celery with Mushrooms and Cream (see page 77)

Vegetable Shepherd's Pie

Illustrated on pages 22-23
Serves 4

Metric·Imperial	American
450 g/1 lb potatoes	1 lb potatoes
225 g/8 oz carrots	½ lb carrots
salt and pepper	salt and pepper
50 g/2 oz margarine	¼ cup margarine
2 medium onions	2 medium onions
100 g/4 oz mushrooms	¼ lb mushrooms
2 tablespoons oil	3 tablespoons oil
½-1 tablespoon yeast extract	¾-1 tablespoon yeast extract
50 g/2 oz peanuts, chopped	½ cup chopped peanuts
1 tablespoon chopped parsley	1 tablespoon chopped parsley
½-1 teaspoon chopped thyme	½-1 teaspoon chopped thyme
2 tablespoons soft breadcrumbs	3 tablespoons fresh soft bread crumbs
1 tablespoon tomato ketchup	1 tablespoon tomato ketchup

Peel the potatoes and the carrots, cook separately in well-seasoned boiling water until just tender. Strain. Mash the potatoes with half the margarine. Chop the cooked carrots. Peel and slice or chop the onions, wash the mushrooms.

Heat the remaining margarine with the oil in a pan. Fry the onions and mushrooms steadily until soft; do not allow the onions to brown. Add the yeast extract, carrots and remaining ingredients, except the potatoes. Spoon into a flameproof dish, top with the potatoes and brown under the grill or heat through in the centre of a moderately hot oven (200°C, 400°F, Gas Mark 6).

Freezing This freezes well. Use within 3 months.

Variation

Omit the peanuts and use a generous amount of cooked peas or other vegetable rich in protein.

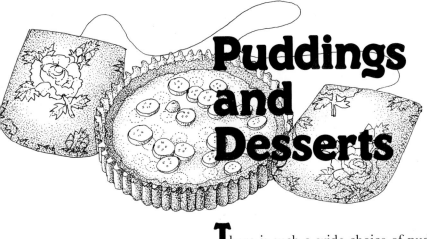

Puddings and Desserts

There is such a wide choice of puddings and desserts, that I have concentrated on the particular recipes which will add nutritional value to the whole meal. As you will see, I have made good use of the modern muesli, of eggs, milk, nuts and fruit. Most of these recipes can be adapted to use other flavourings or other fruits, so will be a stand-by throughout the whole year.

Scottish Custard

Serves 4

Metric·Imperial	American
4 eggs	4 eggs
25-40 g/1-1½ oz sugar	3 tablespoons sugar
2 tablespoons brandy or whisky	3 tablespoons brandy or whisky
600 ml/1 pint milk	2½ cups milk
25 g/1 oz candied lemon or orange peel, chopped	3 tablespoons chopped candied lemon or orange peel
3 tablespoons orange marmalade	¼ cup orange marmalade

Beat the eggs with the sugar and brandy or whisky. Warm the milk and gradually whisk on to the eggs. Pour or strain into 4 individual or 1 large ovenproof dish. Stand in a tin containing cold water (to prevent the custard curdling). Sprinkle the lemon or orange peel on top and add the marmalade. It is better to do this last as it makes sure peel and preserve are more evenly distributed.

Bake for about 40 minutes (if using small dishes) or 1¼-1½ hours (for 1 larger dish) in the centre of a cool to moderate oven (150-160°C, 300-325°F, Gas Mark 2-3). Serve hot or cold. If serving cold, the dessert can be topped with whipped cream and small blobs of marmalade.

Summer Muesli

Serves 4

Metric·Imperial	American
50 g/2 oz strawberries	scant ½ cup strawberries
50 g/2 oz grapes	½ cup grapes
25 g/1 oz seedless raisins	3 tablespoons seeded raisins
25 g/1 oz nuts, chopped	¼ cup chopped nuts
1 (439-g/15½-oz) can creamed rice	1 (15½-oz) can creamed rice
25 g/1 oz rolled oats	¼ cup rolled oats

Halve the strawberries and deseed the grapes. Mix all the ingredients together and chill.

Variations

Cook 50 g/2 oz (U.S. 4 tablespoons) rice in 600 ml/1 pint (U.S. 2½ cups) milk, or milk and cream, and 50 g/2 oz (U.S. ¼ cup) sugar until thick and creamy and use in place of the canned rice.

Winter muesli Use diced cooked and well drained rhubarb instead of strawberries and chopped dates in place of raisins.

Muesli

Illustrated opposite

To make your own muesli, mix rolled oats with dried fruit, chopped nuts and sweeten with honey or black treacle. You can add chopped dessert apple, lemon or orange juice and moisten the mixture with milk or yogurt. There are however excellent commercial products available in packet form to which you can add your own extras.

Muesli is very versatile; the illustration opposite shows the cereal served with milk and fresh strawberries, and there are other recipes using this cereal on page 84 and above.

Rhubarb and Ginger Brown Betty

Illustrated on page 91
Serves 4-6

Metric·Imperial	American
75 g/3 oz butter	¼ cup plus 2 tablespoons butter
225 g/8 oz muesli type cereal	½ lb muesli type cereal
100 g/4 oz demerara sugar	½ cup light brown sugar
1 teaspoon ground ginger	1 teaspoon ground ginger
675 g/1½ lb rhubarb	1½ lb rhubarb

Melt the butter in a large pan, add the cereal, sugar and ginger. Cut the rhubarb into small pieces. Arrange the fruit and cereal mixture in layers in an ovenproof dish, ending with the cereal mixture. Press this down firmly and bake for about 40 minutes in the centre of a moderate oven (180°C, 350°F, Gas Mark 4), until the fruit is soft and the topping crisp and brown.

Freezing This freezes well for 3 months; heat very slowly from the frozen state.

Variations

Add a little extra sugar to the rhubarb layers.

Use other fruit instead of rhubarb.

Muesli (see above); Muesli Fruit Flan (see page 84)

Banana and Honey Flan

Illustrated on page 91
Serves 6

Metric · Imperial	American
75 g/3 oz butter	½ cup plus 2 tablespoons butter
3 tablespoons clear honey	¼ cup clear honey
25 g/1 oz demerara sugar	2 tablespoons light brown sugar
225 g/8 oz muesli type cereal	½ lb muesli type cereal
For the filling	**For the filling**
2 teaspoons Agar-Agar	2 teaspoons Agar-Agar
juice ½ lemon	juice ½ lemon
1 tablespoon water	1 tablespoon water
100 g/4 oz cream cheese	½ cup cream cheese
3 bananas	3 bananas
1 tablespoon clear honey	1 tablespoon honey
To decorate	**To decorate**
1 large banana, sliced	1 large banana, sliced

Melt the butter, honey and sugar in a saucepan over a low heat, then boil gently for half a minute. Remove from the heat and stir in the cereal. Place a greased 18-20-cm/7-8-inch flan ring on an upturned greased baking tray. Line the flan ring with the mixture, and press well to base and sides. Bake in the centre of a moderate oven (180°C, 350°F, Gas Mark 4) for 8-10 minutes, until golden brown, then remove from the oven and leave until cold. When the mixture is firm, gradually ease the flan on to a serving plate and remove the flan ring.

To make the filling soak the Agar-Agar in the lemon juice and water for 10 minutes, and then dissolve over a pan of boiling water. Beat the cream cheese until soft, add the mashed bananas, honey and Agar-Agar mixture. Turn into the prepared flan case and leave in the refrigerator until set. Decorate with banana slices.

Freezing This freezes well for 1 month.

Variation
Muesli fruit flan Make the flan as above and fill with mixed fresh or cooked fruit, as shown in the illustration on the jacket, and on page 83. Decorate with blanched almonds or with a glaze made by heating 4 tablespoons (U.S. ⅓ cup) redcurrant jelly and 2 tablespoons (U.S. 3 tablespoons) water together. Cool slightly, then brush over the fruit.

Sugarbaby Party Bowl

Illustrated on page 86
Serves 6

Metric · Imperial	American
1 watermelon	1 watermelon
1 small honeydew or Ogen melon	1 small honeydew or cantaloupe melon
3 oranges	3 oranges
1 grapefruit	1 grapefruit
2 tablespoons sherry	3 tablespoons sherry
To decorate	**To decorate**
sprigs mint	sprigs mint
lemons or limes	lemons or limes

Cut a slice from the top of the watermelon, then cut the edges in a Van-dyke fashion, as illustrated. Halve a small honeydew or Ogen melon. Scoop out the seeds from both melons and cut the pulp in balls with a melon baller, or dice neatly. Cut away the peel and pith from the oranges and grapefruit and cut the fruit in segments, discarding all skin and pips. Mix the fruits together, spoon back into the watermelon case and sprinkle with the sherry. Chill well. Top with mint sprigs and slices of lemons or limes.

Metric · Imperial	American
2 eggs	2 eggs
300 ml/½ pint milk	1¼ cups milk
50 g/2 oz sugar	¼ cup sugar
¼-½ teaspoon vanilla essence	¼-½ teaspoon vanilla extract
300 ml/½ pint double cream	1¼ cups heavy cream

Home-made Ice Cream

Serves 4-6

Separate the eggs. Whisk the yolks, milk, sugar and vanilla essence in a basin or the top of a double saucepan. Stand over a pan of hot, but not boiling, water, cook gently, stirring well until the mixture coats the back of a wooden spoon. Allow to cool, stirring occasionally to stop a skin forming. Whip the cream, fold into the cold custard, freeze lightly. Whisk the egg whites, fold into the half-frozen mixture. Return to the freezer or freezing compartment of the refrigerator.

Freezing Freeze on normal setting in a freezer or 3-star refrigerator.

Variations

Add coffee or chocolate or fruit purée to the mixture (see also below). Mix a little muesli into the half-frozen ice cream before adding the egg whites.

Blackcurrant Ice Cream

Illustrated on page 87
Serves 4

The packet dessert topping is an excellent basis for home-made ice creams. The illustration on page 87 shows ice cream made as follows:

Whisk a 44-g/1½-oz packet of dessert topping with 150 ml/¼ pint (U.S. ⅔ cup) milk until light and fluffy. Blend in bottled blackcurrant syrup to taste (this is an excellent source of vitamin C). Put into a freezing tray and freeze until firm in a freezer or the freezing compartment of a refrigerator. Top the ice cream with fresh, cooked, canned or frozen blackcurrants.

Metric · Imperial	American
2 eggs	2 eggs
600 ml/1 pint milk	2½ cups milk
100 g/4 oz castor sugar	½ cup superfine sugar
2 teaspoons grated orange rind	2 teaspoons grated orange rind
To decorate	**To decorate**
2 medium oranges	2 medium oranges

Orange Floating Islands

Serves 4

Separate the yolks from the whites of the eggs, add a little of the milk to the yolks and cover to prevent a skin forming on them. Put the remaining milk, 25 g/1 oz (U.S. 2 tablespoons) sugar and the grated orange rind into a large shallow saucepan or frying pan. Whisk the egg whites until very stiff. Gradually whisk in half the remaining sugar, then fold in the rest. Drop balls of this meringue on top of the hot milk, poach for 1½-2 minutes; turn with a perforated spoon, poach on the second side. Never let the milk boil too quickly, otherwise the meringue will be tough. Lift the meringue balls off the hot milk and drain on a sieve. Strain the milk over the beaten yolks, then, in a double saucepan or basin over hot water, cook, stirring until a thickened custard sauce. Cool.

Pour into a shallow glass bowl and top with the meringue balls. Cut the peel and pith away from the oranges, divide into segments and skin them. Decorate the dessert with the fresh orange segments.

Overleaf left: Sugarbaby Party Bowl (see page 84)
Overleaf right: Blackcurrant Ice Cream (see above)

Vienna Apple Meringue

Illustrated on page 90
Serves 4-6

Metric·Imperial	American
75 g/3 oz seedless raisins	½ cup seeded raisins
50 g/2 oz soft breadcrumbs	1 cup fresh soft bread crumbs
600 ml/1 pint thick sweetened apple purée	2½ cups thick sweetened applesauce
50 g/2 oz blanched almonds, chopped	½ cup chopped blanched almonds
2 eggs	2 eggs
For the meringue	**For the meringue**
50 g/2 oz castor sugar	¼ cup superfine sugar
25 g/1 oz blanched almonds	¼ cup blanched almonds

Cover the raisins with cold water, bring to the boil, leave to stand for 5 minutes, drain well. This makes the fruit more plump and juicy. Mix the breadcrumbs, apple purée, almonds and raisins together. Separate the eggs (saving the whites for meringue topping), whisk the yolks and stir into breadcrumb mixture. Pour into 1 large or 4-6 small buttered ovenproof dishes. Cook in the centre of a moderate oven (160°C, 325°F, Gas Mark 3), 35 minutes for a large pudding or 15 minutes for individual puddings.

Whisk the egg whites until stiff enough to form peaks, fold in the sugar and spoon or pipe this on top of the breadcrumb mixture. Spike the meringue with flaked whole or halved almonds. Bake in the centre of the moderate oven, 20-25 minutes for the larger pudding and about 15 minutes for the smaller ones.

Freezing This dessert freezes well. Use within 2 months. Serve as soon as defrosted otherwise meringue will lose its crispness.

Variations

Substitute apricot or rhubarb purée for the apple purée.

Apricot and Almond Plait

Serves 6

Cut 225 g/8 oz (U.S. ½ lb) dried unsoaked apricots into small pieces with kitchen scissors. Put into a basin, cover with boiling water and leave for 12 hours. Drain off the liquid (this could be served as a sauce with the plait or put into a mould). Blend the apricots with 2 tablespoons (U.S. 3 tablespoons) honey and 1 tablespoon lemon juice. Add 50 g/2 oz (U.S. ½ cup) blanched chopped almonds.

Make shortcrust pastry with 225 g/8 oz (U.S. 2 cups) flour, etc. (see page 37). Roll out the pastry to make a large oblong shape, mark lightly into three portions lengthways. Make diagonal cuts on the two outer portions. Spread the centre third with the apricot and almond mixture. Fold over the strips from the outer portions to make a plaited effect. Seal the edges, brush with beaten egg or a little milk and lift on to a baking tray.

Bake in the centre of a moderately hot oven (200°C, 400°F, Gas Mark 6) for 25-30 minutes, reducing the heat slightly after 15 minutes to prevent the pastry becoming over-brown. Allow the plait to cool.

Combine 100 g/4 oz (U.S. scant 1 cup) sifted icing sugar with 1 tablespoon lemon juice. Spread the icing on the plait and decorate with glacé cherries and blanched almonds.

Freezing Open freeze then wrap; use within 3 months.

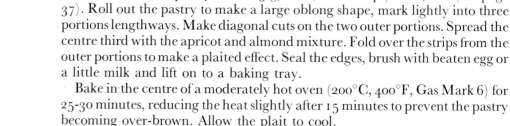

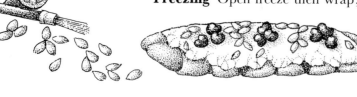

Grapefruit Cheesecake

Serves 6

Metric·Imperial For the base	American For the base
75 g/3 oz butter	¼ cup plus 2 tablespoons butter
3 tablespoons golden syrup	¼ cup corn syrup
175 g/6 oz bran flakes	6 cups bran flakes
For the filling	**For the filling**
2 teaspoons Agar-Agar	2 teaspoons Agar-Agar
2 tablespoons water	3 tablespoons water
225 g/8 oz cottage cheese	1 cup cottage cheese
150 ml/¼ pint double cream	⅔ cup heavy cream
juice of 1 grapefruit	juice of 1 grapefruit
25 g/1 oz castor sugar	2 tablespoons superfine sugar
To decorate	**To decorate**
1 grapefruit	1 grapefruit

Melt the butter and golden syrup in a saucepan. Stir in the bran flakes, and press into an 18-cm/7-inch flan dish, reserving a little of the mixture for decoration. Bake in the centre of a moderate oven (180°C, 350°F, Gas Mark 4) for 10 minutes. Cool.

Soften the Agar-Agar in the water for 10 minutes and then stand over a saucepan of boiling water until dissolved. Allow to cool. Sieve the cottage cheese, then mix with the cream, grapefruit juice and sugar. Whisk in the Agar-Agar. Allow to begin to set; spoon into the flan ring and spread level on top. Place in the refrigerator to set.

Cut away the peel and pith from the grapefruit, cut into segments and arrange these on top of the cheesecake with a border of the remaining bran flake mixture.

Freezing Most cheesecakes freeze well. Use this particular one within 2 months. Freeze the grapefruit topping separately.

Variation
Use orange juice and segments instead of grapefruit.

Quick Mocha Soufflé

Serves 4

Metric·Imperial	American
1 (411-g/14½-oz) can custard	1 (14½-oz) can custard
2 tablespoons drinking chocolate powder	3 tablespoons drinking chocolate powder
5 teaspoons coffee essence	5 teaspoons strong coffee
4 eggs	4 eggs

Put the custard into a basin, add the chocolate and coffee essence. Separate the eggs and beat the yolks into the custard. Whisk the whites in a separate bowl and fold into the mocha mixture. Spoon into an 18-cm/7-inch greased soufflé dish and bake in the centre of a moderate oven (160°C, 325°F, Gas Mark 3) for 50 minutes, until lightly set.

Variations
Speedy chocolate soufflé Omit the coffee essence and use an extra tablespoon of drinking chocolate powder.

Make a thick custard with 2-3 egg yolks and 450 ml/¾ pint (U.S. scant 2 cups) milk and 50 g/2 oz (U.S. ¼ cup) sugar, instead of using canned custard.

Overleaf left: Vienna Apple Meringue (see page 88)
Overleaf right: Banana and Honey Flan (see page 84); Rhubarb and Ginger Brown Betty (see page 82); Wheatmeal Plait (see page 93)

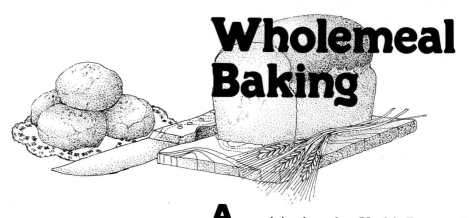

Wholemeal Baking

As explained under Useful Facts and Figures, this book does not try to dictate just what kind of fat, flour, etc., you will use. If you are a vegetarian you will choose vegetarian fats. Whether or not you are a vegetarian, you may well like to use wholemeal flour in all your cooking. The results are good, and the flavour is delicious.

In Britain one can purchase both wholemeal flour (100% whole wheat) and wheatmeal flour (80-90% extraction). The latter gives lighter cakes. Sift wholemeal or wheatmeal flour to lighten; you may find some of the bran separates during this process and remains in the sieve; add this back for it is an important food.

Wholemeal and wheatmeal flours tend to absorb a little more liquid in mixing, which means the food may take a slightly longer cooking time.

Wholemeal and wheatmeal flours have the same thickening properties, so use these to make sauces; you may at first be a little worried about the slightly darker colour, but the delicious nutty flavour will compensate for that. There are points about making pastry with wholemeal flour on page 37.

We are told today that the civilised World suffers from a shortage of fibre in our refined foods; this type of flour does a great deal to combat that.

Gouda Tea Bread

Illustrated on page 19
Makes 6 rolls

Metric·Imperial	American
225 g/8 oz plain wholemeal flour	2 cups all-purpose wholewheat flour
225 g/8 oz plain flour	2 cups all-purpose flour
4½ teaspoons baking powder	4½ teaspoons baking powder
½-1 teaspoon salt	½-1 teaspoon salt
½-1 teaspoon paprika	½-1 teaspoon paprika
4 tablespoons piccalilli	⅓ cup sweet mustard pickles
225 g/8 oz Gouda cheese, grated	2 cups grated Gouda cheese
1 large egg	1 large egg
approximately 300 ml/½ pint milk	approximately 1¼ cups milk

Sift the flours, baking powder, salt and paprika together. Chop the piccalilli very finely, add to the flour with nearly all the grated cheese. Beat the egg with most of the milk, use nearly all of this to bind the ingredients together (save a small amount of egg and milk for glazing the bread). The dough should be a soft elastic consistency, that you can handle; you may find you need to add the last of the milk. Knead the dough lightly until smooth, then divide into 6 equal sized pieces and form these into rolls. Put on a baking tray to form a circle, leaving a space between each roll. Brush with the last of the egg and milk and top with the remaining grated cheese.

Bake in the centre of a hot oven (220°C, 425°F, Gas Mark 7) for about 20 minutes, then lower the heat slightly and continue cooking for another 10-15 minutes. Serve hot or cold with soups or salads. (See the illustration on page 19).

Freezing This bread freezes well after cooking; use within 6 weeks.

Wheatmeal Plait

Illustrated on page 91

Makes 1 large loaf

Metric·Imperial	American
450 ml/¾ pint water	2 cups water
25 g/1 oz fresh yeast or 15 g/½ oz dried yeast	1 cake compressed yeast or ½ oz active dry yeast
1 teaspoon brown sugar	1 teaspoon brown sugar
575 g/1¼ lb wheatmeal plain flour	5 cups wheatmeal all-purpose flour
½-1 teaspoon salt	½-1 teaspoon salt
25 g/1 oz butter or margarine	2 tablespoons butter or margarine
75 g/3 oz bran or sultana bran	generous ½ cup bran or sultana bran
To glaze	**To glaze**
little milk	little milk
few poppy seeds	few poppy seeds

Heat the water until it feels comfortably warm to the touch. If using fresh yeast cream this with the sugar, then add the water. If using dried yeast dissolve the sugar in the water, sprinkle the yeast on top. Allow to stand in a warm place for about 15 minutes, until the surface becomes frothy.

Sift the flour and salt, rub in the butter or margarine, then add the bran or sultana bran and the yeast liquid. Knead the bread dough on a lightly floured board until no impression is left when pressed with a lightly floured finger. Return to the mixing bowl or put into a large greased polythene bag and allow to prove for 1 hour. Knead again. Divide the dough into 3 portions and knead until each piece becomes a roll about 30 cm/12 inches long. Plait the rolls together loosely and seal the ends. Lift on to a lightly greased baking tray. Brush with a little milk. Sprinkle with poppy seeds and allow to prove until almost double the original size. Bake in the centre of a hot oven (220°C, 425°F, Gas Mark 7) for 20 minutes, then reduce the heat to moderately hot (190°C, 375°F, Gas Mark 5) for approximately 15-20 minutes. To test if cooked, knock the loaf on the bottom and it should sound hollow.

Freezing Cool, freeze, then wrap. Use within 6 weeks.

Potato Bread Rolls

Makes 10

Reconstitute a 64-g/2¼-oz packet of dehydrated potato pieces as directed, and cool. Sift 225 g/8 oz (U.S. 2 cups) self-raising wholemeal flour with 2 teaspoons baking powder and a pinch of salt, rub in 50 g/2 oz (U.S. ¼ cup) margarine. Mix in the potato, and gradually add about 4 tablespoons (U.S. 5 tablespoons) milk to give a soft pliable dough. Divide into 10 portions and shape into batons, rounds or small cottage loaves. Place on a greased and floured baking tray. Bake just above the centre of a moderately hot oven (200°C, 400°F, Gas Mark 6) until golden brown and firm, about 30 minutes.

Index